MW00891610

ROMAN CATHOLIC MISSAL CATHOLIC SUNDAY AND DAILY MASS READING 2025

LITURGICAL YEAR C DEC, JAN AND FEB

BOOK 1 OF 4. [Q1]

Edited by
AVA SINCLAIR

CONTENTS

FOREWORD

The following readings for each week day and weekend day provide a deeper connection to the Bible in both worship and personal devotion by offering daily reading references for the entire Year C of the three-year cycle in the Revised Common Lectionary. *This is book one of four.* Readings cover every day of the year and are designed to complement the Sunday and festival scriptures. From Thursday to Saturday, the readings prepare you for the upcoming Sunday, while those from Monday to Wednesday help you reflect on and absorb the teachings from the previous Sunday's worship. ***Other books in the series include:***

BOOK 1: Dec 24, Jan 25, Feb 25
BOOK 2: Mar, Apr, May
BOOK 3: Jun, Jul, Aug
BOOK 4: Sep, Oct, Nov

The Annunciation (1655-1660)
Bartholomé Esteban Murillo

LITURGICAL YEAR C

Liturgical Year C
Weekday, Saturday and Sunday Mass Readings
and Resources from
Advent 2024 to Advent 2025

The 2025 **Liturgical Year C** begins on the
First Sunday of Advent, December 1, 2024.

PRIMARY CELEBRATIONS OF THE LITURGICAL YEAR

First Sunday of Advent - December 1, 2024
Ash Wednesday - March 5, 2025
Easter Sunday - April 20, 2025
The Ascension of the Lord [Thursday] - May 29, 2025
Pentecost Sunday - June 8, 2025
The Most Holy Body and Blood of Christ - June 22, 2025
First Sunday of Advent - November 30, 2025

LITURGY OF THE HOURS

Dec. 1, 2024 – Jan. 12, 2025
Advent, Christmas Vol. I

Jan. 13 – Mar. 4, 2025
Weeks 1 to 8, Ordinary Time Vol. III

Mar. 5 – June 8, 2025
Lent, Triduum, Easter Vol. II

June 9 – Aug. 2, 2025
Weeks 10 to 17, Ordinary Time Vol. III

Aug. 3 – Nov. 29, 2025
Weeks 18 to 34, Ordinary Time Vol. IV

Nov. 30, 2025 – Jan. 11, 2026
Advent, Christmas Vol. I

SUNDAYS, FEAST DAYS AND LITURGICAL COLORS

Date, Day /Feast, Liturgical Color

December 1, 2024, First Sunday of Advent, Blue or Purple

December 8, 2024, Second Sunday of Advent, Blue or Purple

December 15, 2024, Third Sunday of Advent, Blue or Purple

December 22, 2024, Fourth Sunday of Advent, Blue or Purple

December 24, 2024, Nativity of Our Lord (Christmas Eve), White

December 25, 2024, Nativity of Our Lord (Christmas Day), White

December 29, 2024, First Sunday of Christmas, White

January 5, 2025, Second Sunday of Christmas, White

January 6, 2025, Feast of the Epiphany, White

January 12, 2025, Baptism of Our Lord, White

January 19, 2025, Second Sunday after the Epiphany, Green

January 26, 2025, Third Sunday after the Epiphany Green

~

February 2, 2025, Fourth Sunday after the Epiphany, Green

February 9, 2025, Fifth Sunday after the Epiphany, Green

February 16, 2025, Sixth Sunday after the Epiphany, Green

February 23, 2025, Seventh Sunday after the Epiphany, Green

~

March 2, 2025, Transfiguration, White

March 5, 2025, Ash Wednesday, Purple

March 9, 2025, First Sunday in Lent, Purple

March 16, 2025, Second Sunday in Lent, Purple

March 23, 2025, Third Sunday in Lent, Purple

March 30, 2025, Fourth Sunday in Lent, Purple

~

April 6, 2025, Fifth Sunday in Lent, Purple

April 13, 2025, Palm Sunday, Scarlet or Purple

April 17, 2025, Maundy Thursday, Scarlet or Purple

April 18, 2025, Good Friday, Black or None

April 20, 2025, Resurrection of Our Lord (Easter Sunrise), White

April 20, 2025, Resurrection of Our Lord (Easter Day), White

April 27, 2025, Second Sunday of Easter, White

~

May 4, 2025, Third Sunday of Easter, White

May 11, 2024, Fourth Sunday of Easter, White

May 18, 2025 Fifth Sunday of Easter, White

May 25, 2025, Sixth Sunday of Easter, White

May 29, 2025, Ascension of the Lord. White

∿

June 1, 2025. Seventh Sunday of Easter, White

June 8, 2025, Day of Pentecost, Red

June 15, 2025, The Holy Trinity, White

June 22, 2025, Second Sunday after Pentecost, Green

June 29, 2025, Third Sunday after Pentecost, Green

∿

July 6, 2025, Fourth Sunday after Pentecost, Green

July 13, 2025, Fifth Sunday after Pentecost, Green

July 20, 2025 Sixth Sunday after Pentecost, Green

July 27, 2025, Seventh Sunday after Pentecost, Green

August 3, 2025, Eighth Sunday after Pentecost, Green

August 10, 2025, Ninth Sunday after Pentecost, Green

August 17, 2025, Tenth Sunday after Pentecost, Green

August 24, 2025, Eleventh Sunday after Pentecost, Green

August 31, 2025, Twelfth Sunday after Pentecost, Green

∿

September 7, 2025, Thirteenth Sunday after Pentecost, Green

September 14, 2025 Fourteenth Sunday after Pentecost, Green

September 21. 2025, Fifteenth Sunday after Pentecost, Green

September 28, 2025, Sixteenth Sunday after Pentecost, Green

∿

October 5, 2025, Seventeenth Sunday after Pentecost, Green

October 12, 2025, Eighteenth Sunday after Pentecost, Green

October 19, 2025 Nineteenth Sunday after Pentecost. Green

October 26, 2025, Reformation Sunday, Red

∾

November 2, 2025, All Saints Day, White

November 9, 2025, Twenty-second Sunday after Pentecost, Green

November 16, 2025, Twenty-third Sunday after Pentecost, Green

November 23, 2025, Christ the King, White

November 27, 2025, Thanksgiving Day (USA), Green (or White)

Adoration of the Magi (1475)
Sandro Botticelli

DECEMBER 2024

SUNDAY DECEMBER 1, 2024
FIRST SUNDAY OF ADVENT

First Reading: Jeremiah 33: 14-16

Responsorial Psalm: Psalms 25: 4-5, 8-9, 10, 14

Second Reading: First Thessalonians 3: 12 – 4: 2

Alleluia: Psalms 85: 8

Gospel: Luke 21: 25-28, 34-36

First Reading: Jeremiah 33: 14-16

14 Behold the days come, saith the Lord, that I will perform the good word that I have spoken to the house of Israel, and to the house of Juda.

15 In those days, and at that time, I will make the bud of justice to spring forth unto David, and he shall do judgment and justice in the earth.

16 In those days shall Juda be saved, and Jerusalem shall dwell securely: and this is the name that they shall call him, The Lord our just one.

Responsorial Psalm: Psalms 25: 4-5, 8-9, 10, 14

R. (1b) To you, O Lord, I lift my soul.

4 Let all them be confounded that act unjust things without cause. shew, O Lord, thy ways to me, and teach me thy paths.

5 Direct me in thy truth, and teach me; for thou art God my Saviour; and on thee have I waited all the day long.

R. To you, O Lord, I lift my soul.

8 The Lord is sweet and righteous: therefore he will give a law to sinners in the way.

9 He will guide the mild in judgment: he will teach the meek his ways.

R. To you, O Lord, I lift my soul.

10 All the ways of the Lord are mercy and truth, to them that seek after his covenant and his testimonies.

R. To you, O Lord, I lift my soul.

14 The Lord is a firmament to them that fear him: and his covenant shall be made manifest to them.

R. To you, O Lord, I lift my soul.

Second Reading: First Thessalonians 3: 12 – 4: 2

12 And may the Lord multiply you, and make you abound in charity towards one another, and towards all men: as we do also towards you,

13 To confirm your hearts without blame, in holiness, before God and our Father, at the coming of our Lord Jesus Christ, with all his saints. Amen.

4:1 For the rest therefore, brethren, we pray and beseech you in the Lord Jesus, that as you have received from us, how you ought to walk, and to please God, so also you would walk, that you may abound the more.

2 For you know what precepts I have given to you by the Lord Jesus.

Alleluia: Psalms 85: 8

R. Alleluia, alleluia.

8 Show us, Lord, your love; and grant us your salvation.

R. Alleluia, alleluia.

Gospel: Luke 21: 25-28, 34-36

25 And there shall be signs in the sun, and in the moon, and in the stars; and upon the earth distress of nations, by reason of the confusion of the roaring of the sea and of the waves;

26 Men withering away for fear, and expectation of what shall come upon the whole world. For the powers of heaven shall be moved;

27 And then they shall see the Son of man coming in a cloud, with great power and majesty.

28 But when these things begin to come to pass, look up, and lift up your heads, because your redemption is at hand.

34 And take heed to yourselves, lest perhaps your hearts be overcharged with surfeiting and drunkenness, and the cares of this life, and that day come upon you suddenly.

35 For as a snare shall it come upon all that sit upon the face of the whole earth.

36 Watch ye, therefore, praying at all times, that you may be accounted worthy to escape all these things that are to come, and to stand before the Son of man.

∼

MONDAY DECEMBER 2, 2024

First Reading: Isaiah 2: 1-5

Responsorial Psalm: Psalms 122: 1-2, 3-4b, 4cd-5, 6-7, 8-9

Alleluia: Psalms 80: 4

Gospel: Matthew 8: 5-11

First Reading: Isaiah 2: 1-5

1 The word that Isaias the son of Amos saw, concerning Juda and Jerusalem.

2 And in the last days the mountain of the house of the Lord shall be prepared on the top of mountains, and it shall be exalted above the hills, and all nations shall flow unto it.

3 And many people shall go, and say: Come and let us go up to the mountain of the Lord, and to the house of the God of Jacob, and he will teach us his ways, and we will walk in his paths: for the law shall come forth from Sion, and the word of the Lord from Jerusalem.

4 And he shall judge the Gentiles, and rebuke many people: and they shall turn their swords into plough shares, and their spears into sickles: nation shall not lift up sword against nation, neither shall they be exercised any more to war.

5 O house of Jacob, come ye, and let us walk in the light of the Lord.

Responsorial Psalm: Psalms 122: 1-2, 3-4b, 4cd-5, 6-7, 8-9

R. Let us go rejoicing to the house of the Lord.

1 I rejoiced at the things that were said to me: We shall go into the house of the Lord.

2 Our feet were standing in thy courts, O Jerusalem.

R. Let us go rejoicing to the house of the Lord.

3 Jerusalem, which is built as a city, which is compact together.

4ab For thither did the tribes go up, the tribes of the Lord.

R. Let us go rejoicing to the house of the Lord.

4cd The testimony of Israel, to praise the name of the Lord.

5 Because their seats have sat in judgment, seats upon the house of David.

R. Let us go rejoicing to the house of the Lord.

6 Pray ye for the things that are for the peace of Jerusalem: and abundance for them that love thee.

7 Let peace be in thy strength: and abundance in thy towers.

R. Let us go rejoicing to the house of the Lord.

8 For the sake of my brethren, and of my neighbours, I spoke peace of thee.

9 Because of the house of the Lord our God, I have sought good things for thee.

R. Let us go rejoicing to the house of the Lord.

Alleluia: Psalms 80: 4

R. Alleluia, alleluia.

4 Come and save us, LORD our God; let your face shine upon us, that we may be saved.

R. Alleluia, alleluia.

Gospel: Matthew 8: 5-11

5 And when he had entered into Capharnaum, there came to him a centurion, beseeching him,

6 And saying, Lord, my servant lieth at home sick of the palsy, and is grieviously tormented.

7 And Jesus saith to him: I will come and heal him.

8 And the centurion making answer, said: Lord, I am not worthy that thou shouldst enter under my roof: but only say the word, and my servant shall be healed.

9 For I also am a man subject to authority, having under me soldiers; and I say to this, Go, and he goeth, and to another, Come, and he cometh, and to my servant, Do this, and he doeth it.

10 And Jesus hearing this, marvelled; and said to them that followed him: Amen I say to you, I have not found so great faith in Israel.

11 And I say to you that many shall come from the east and the west, and shall sit down with Abraham, and Isaac, and Jacob in the kingdom of heaven.

TUESDAY DECEMBER 3, 2024

First Reading: Isaiah 11: 1-10

Responsorial Psalm: Psalms 72: 1-2, 7-8, 12-13, 17

Gospel: Luke 10: 21-24

First Reading: Isaiah 11: 1-10

1 And there shall come forth a rod out of the root of Jesse, and a flower shall rise up out of his root.

2 And the spirit of the Lord shall rest upon him: the spirit of wisdom, and of understanding, the spirit of counsel, and of fortitude, the spirit of knowledge, and of godliness.

3 And he shall be filled with the spirit of the fear of the Lord. He shall not judge according to the sight of the eyes, nor reprove according to the hearing of the ears.

4 But he shall judge the poor with justice, and shall reprove with equity for the meek of the earth: land he shall strike the earth with the rod of his mouth, and with the breath of his lips he shall slay the wicked.

5 And justice shall be the girdle of his loins: and faith the girdle of his reins.

6 The wolf shall dwell with the lamb: and the leopard shall lie down with the kid: the calf and the lion, and the sheep shall abide together, and a little child shall lead them.

7 The calf and the bear shall feed: their young ones shall rest together: and the lion shall eat straw like the ox.

8 And the sucking child shall play on the hole of the asp: and the weaned child shall thrust his hand into the den of the basilisk.

9 They shall not hurt, nor shall they kill in all my holy mountain, for the earth is filled with the knowledge of the Lord, as the covering waters of the sea.

10 In that day the root of Jesse, who standeth for an ensign of the people, him the Gentiles shall beseech, and his sepulchre shall be glorious.

Responsorial Psalm: Psalms 72: 1-2, 7-8, 12-13, 17

R. (7) Justice shall flourish in his time, and fullness of peace for ever.

2 Give to the king thy judgment, O God: and to the king's son thy justice: To judge thy people with justice, and thy poor with judgment.

R. Justice shall flourish in his time, and fullness of peace for ever.

21

7 In his days shall justice spring up, and abundance of peace, till the moon be taken sway.

8 And he shall rule from sea to sea, and from the river unto the ends of the earth.

R. Justice shall flourish in his time, and fullness of peace for ever.

12 For he shall deliver the poor from the mighty: and the needy that had no helper.

13 He shall spare the poor and needy: and he shall save the souls of the poor.

R. Justice shall flourish in his time, and fullness of peace for ever.

17 Let his name be blessed for evermore: his name continueth before the sun. And in him shall all the tribes of the earth be blessed: all nations shall magnify him.

R. Justice shall flourish in his time, and fullness of peace for ever.

Alleluia

R. Alleluia, alleluia.

Behold, our Lord shall come with power; he will enlighten the eyes of his servants.

R. Alleluia, alleluia.

Gospel: Luke 10: 21-24

21 In that same hour, he rejoiced in the Holy Ghost, and said: I confess to thee, O Father, Lord of heaven and earth, because thou hast hidden these things from the wise and prudent, and hast revealed them to little ones. Yea, Father, for so it hath seemed good in thy sight.

22 All things are delivered to me by my Father; and no one knoweth who the Son is, but the Father; and who the Father is, but the Son, and to whom the Son will reveal him.

23 And turning to his disciples, he said: Blessed are the eyes that see the things which you see.

24 For I say to you, that many prophets and kings have desired to see the things that you see, and have not seen them; and to hear the things that you hear, and have not heard them.

~

WEDNESDAY DECEMBER 4, 2024

First Reading: Isaiah 25: 6-10a

Responsorial Psalm: Psalms 23: 1-3a, 3b-4, 5, 6

Gospel: Matthew 15: 29-37

First Reading: Isaiah 25: 6-10a

6 And the Lord of hosts shall make unto all people in this mountain, a feast of fat things, a feast of wine, of fat things full of marrow, of wine purified from the lees.

7 And he shall destroy in this mountain the face of the bond with which all people were tied, and the web that he began over all nations.

8 He shall cast death down headlong for ever: and the Lord God shall wipe away tears from every face, and the reproach of his people he shall take away from off the whole earth: for the Lord hath spoken it.

9 And they shall say in that day: Lo, this is our God, we have waited for him, and he will save us: this is the Lord, we have patiently waited for him, we shall rejoice and be joyfull in his salvation.

10a For the hand of the Lord shall rest in this mountain.

Responsorial Psalm: Psalms 23: 1-3a, 3b-4, 5, 6

R. (6cd) I shall live in the house of the Lord all the days of my life.

1 The Lord ruleth me: and I shall want nothing.

2 He hath set me in a place of pasture. He hath brought me up, on the water of refreshment:

3a He hath converted my soul.

R. I shall live in the house of the Lord all the days of my life.

3b He hath led me on the paths of justice, for his own name's sake.

4 For though I should walk in the midst of the shadow of death, I will fear no evils, for thou art with me. Thy rod and thy staff, they have comforted me.

R. I shall live in the house of the Lord all the days of my life.

5 Thou hast prepared a table before me against them that afflict me. Thou hast anointed my head with oil; and my chalice which inebriateth me, how goodly is it!

R. I shall live in the house of the Lord all the days of my life.

6 And thy mercy will follow me all the days of my life. And that I may dwell in the house of the Lord unto length of days.

R. I shall live in the house of the Lord all the days of my life.

Alleluia

R. Alleluia, alleluia.

Behold, the Lord comes to save his people; blessed are those prepared to meet him.

R. Alleluia, alleluia.

Gospel: Matthew 15: 29-37

29 And when Jesus had passed away from thence, he came nigh the sea of Galilee. And going up into a mountain, he sat there.

30 And there came to him great multitudes, having with them the dumb, the blind, the lame, the maimed, and many others: and they cast them down at his feet, and he healed them:

31 So that the multitudes marvelled seeing the dumb speak, the lame walk, and the blind see: and they glorified the God of Israel.

32 And Jesus called together his disciples, and said: I have compassion on the multitudes, because they continue with me now three days, and have not what to eat, and I will not send them away fasting, lest they faint in the way.

33 And the disciples say unto him: Whence then should we have so many loaves in the desert, as to fill so great a multitude?

34 And Jesus said to them: How many loaves have you? But they said: Seven, and a few little fishes.

35 And he commanded the multitude to sit down upon the ground.

36 And taking the seven loaves and the fishes, and giving thanks, he brake, and gave to his disciples, and the disciples to the people.

37 And they did all eat, and had their fill. And they took up seven baskets full, of what remained of the fragments.

～

THURSDAY DECEMBER 5, 2024

First Reading: Isaiah 26: 1-6

Responsorial Psalm: Psalms 118: 1 and 8-9, 19-21, 25-27a

Alleluia: Isaiah 55: 6

Gospel: Matthew 7: 21, 24-27

First Reading: Isaiah 26: 1-6

1 In that day shall this canticle be sung the land of Juda. Sion the city of our strength a saviour, a wall and a bulwark shall be set therein.

2 Open ye the gates, and let the just nation, that keepeth the truth, enter in.

3 The old error is passed away: thou wilt keep peace: peace, because we have hoped in thee.

4 You have hoped in the Lord for evermore, in the Lord God mighty for ever.

5 For he shall bring down them that dwell on high, the high city he shall lay low. He shall bring it down even to the ground, he shall pull it down even to the dust.

6 The foot shall tread it down, the feet of the poor, the steps of the needy.

Responsorial Psalm: Psalms 118: 1 and 8-9, 19-21, 25-27a

R. (26a) Blessed is he who comes in the name of the Lord.

or

R. Alleluia.

1 Give praise to Lord, for he is good: for his mercy endureth for ever.

8 It is good to confide in the Lord, rather than to have confidence in man.

9 It is good to trust in the Lord, rather than to trust in princes.

R. Blessed is he who comes in the name of the Lord.

or

R. Alleluia.

19 Open ye to me the gates of justice: I will go into them, and give praise to the Lord.

20 This is the gate of the Lord, the just shall enter into it.

21 I will give glory to thee because thou hast heard me: and art become my salvation.

R. Blessed is he who comes in the name of the Lord.

or

R. Alleluia.

25 O Lord, save me: O Lord, give good success.

26 Blessed be he that cometh in the name Lord. We have blessed you out of the house of the Lord.

27a The Lord is God, and he hath shone upon us.

R. Blessed is he who comes in the name of the Lord.

or

R. Alleluia.

Alleluia: Isaiah 55: 6

R. Alleluia, alleluia.

6 Seek the LORD while he may be found; call him while he is near.

R. Alleluia, alleluia.

Gospel: Matthew 7: 21, 24-27

21 Not every one that saith to me, Lord, Lord, shall enter into the kingdom of

heaven: but he that doth the will of my Father who is in heaven, he shall enter into the kingdom of heaven.

24 Every one therefore that heareth these my words, and doth them, shall be likened to a wise man that built his house upon a rock,

25 And the rain fell, and the floods came, and the winds blew, and they beat upon that house, and it fell not, for it was founded on a rock.

26 And every one that heareth these my words, and doth them not, shall be like a foolish man that built his house upon the sand,

27 And the rain fell, and the floods came, and the winds blew, and they beat upon that house, and it fell, and great was the fall thereof.

~

FRIDAY DECEMBER 6, 2024

First Reading: Isaiah 29: 17-24

Responsorial Psalm: Psalms 27: 1, 4, 13-14

Gospel: Matthew 9: 27-31

First Reading: Isaiah 29: 17-24

17 Is it not yet a very little while, and Libanus shall be turned into charmel, and charmel shall be esteemed as a forest?

18 And in that day the deaf shall hear the words of the book, and out of darkness and obscurity the eyes of the blind shall see.

19 And the meek shall increase their joy in the Lord, and the poor men shall rejoice in the Holy One of Israel.

20 For he that did prevail hath failed, the scorner is consumed, and they are all cut off that watched for iniquity:

21 That made men sin by word, and supplanted him that reproved them in the gate, and declined in vain from the just.

22 Therefore thus saith the Lord to the house of Jacob, he that redeemed Abraham: Jacob shall not now be confounded, neither shall his countenance now be ashamed:

23 But when he shall see his children, the work of my hands in the midst of him sanctifying my name, and they shall sanctify the Holy One of Jacob, and shall glorify the God of Israel:

24 And they that erred in spirit, shall know understanding, and they that murmured, shall learn the law.

Responsorial Psalm: Psalms 27: 1, 4, 13-14

R. (1a) The Lord is my light and my salvation.

1 The psalm of David before he was anointed. The Lord is my light and my salvation, whom shall I fear? The Lord is the protector of my life: of whom shall I be afraid?

R. The Lord is my light and my salvation.

4 One thing I have asked of the Lord, this will I seek after; that I may dwell in the house of the Lord all the days of my life. That I may see the delight of the Lord, and may visit his temple.

R. The Lord is my light and my salvation.

13 I believe to see the good things of the Lord in the land of the living.

14 Expect the Lord, do manfully, and let thy heart take courage, and wait thou for the Lord.

R. The Lord is my light and my salvation.

Alleluia

R. Alleluia, alleluia.

Behold, our Lord shall come with power; he will enlighten the eyes of his servants.

R. Alleluia, alleluia.

Gospel: Matthew 9: 27-31

27 And as Jesus passed from thence, there followed him two blind men crying out and saying, Have mercy on us, O Son of David.

28 And when he was come to the house, the blind men came to him. And Jesus saith to them, Do you believe, that I can do this unto you? They say to him, Yea, Lord.

29 Then he touched their eyes, saying, According to your faith, be it done unto you.

30 And their eyes were opened, and Jesus strictly charged them, saying, See that no man know this.

31 But they going out, spread his fame abroad in all that country.

∾

SATURDAY DECEMBER 7, 2024

First Reading: Isaiah 30: 19-21, 23-26

Responsorial Psalm: Psalms 147: 1-2, 3-4, 5-6

Alleluia: Isaiah 33: 22

Gospel: Matthew 9: 35 – 10: 1, 5a, 6-8

First Reading: Isaiah 30: 19-21, 23-26

19 For the people of Sion shall dwell in Jerusalem: weeping thou shalt not weep, he will surely have pity on thee: at the voice of thy cry, as soon as he shall hear, he will answer thee.

20 And the Lord will give you spare bread, and short water: and will not cause thy teacher to flee away from thee any more, and thy eyes shall see thy teacher.

21 And thy ears shall hear the word of one admonishing thee behind thy back: This is the way, walk ye in it: and go not aside neither to the right hand, nor to the left.

23 And rain shall be given to thy seed, wheresoever thou shalt sow in the land: and the bread of the corn of the land shall be most plentiful, and fat. The lamb in that day shall feed at large in thy possession:

24 And thy oxen, and the ass colts that till the ground, shall eat mingled provender as it was winnowed in the floor.

25 And there shall be upon every high mountain, and upon every elevated hill rivers of running waters in the day of the slaughter of many, when the tower shall fall.

26 And the light of the moon shall be as the light of the sun, and the light of the sun shall be sevenfold, as the light of seven days: in the day when the Lord shall bind up the wound of his people, and shall heal the stroke of their wound.

Responsorial Psalm: Psalms 147: 1-2, 3-4, 5-6

R. (Isaiah 30:18d) Blessed are all who wait for the Lord.

1 Praise ye the Lord, because psalm is good: to our God be joyful and comely praise.

2 The Lord buildeth up Jerusalem: he will gather together the dispersed of Israel.

R. Blessed are all who wait for the Lord.

3 Who healeth the broken of heart, and bindeth up their bruises.

4 Who telleth the number of the stars: and calleth them all by their names.

R. Blessed are all who wait for the Lord.

5 Great is our Lord, and great is his power: and of his wisdom there is no number.

6 The Lord lifteth up the meek, and bringeth the wicked down even to the ground.

R. Blessed are all who wait for the Lord.

Alleluia: Isaiah 33: 22

R. Alleluia, alleluia.

22 The LORD is our Judge, our Lawgiver, our King; he it is who will save us.

R. Alleluia, alleluia.

Gospel: Matthew 9: 35 – 10: 1, 5a, 6-8

35 And Jesus went about all the cities, and towns, teaching in their synagogues, and preaching the gospel of the kingdom, and healing every disease, and every infirmity.

36 And seeing the multitudes, he had compassion on them: because they were distressed, and lying like sheep that have no shepherd.

37 Then he saith to his disciples, The harvest indeed is great, but the labourers are few.

38 Pray ye therefore the Lord of the harvest, that he send forth labourers into his harvest.

10:1 And having called his twelve disciples together, he gave them power over unclean spirits, to cast them out, and to heal all manner of diseases, and all manner of infirmities.

5a These twelve Jesus sent: commanding them, saying:

6 But go ye rather to the lost sheep of the house of Israel.

7 And going, preach, saying: The kingdom of heaven is at hand.

8 Heal the sick, raise the dead, cleanse the lepers, cast out devils: freely have you received, freely give.

∽

SUNDAY DECEMBER 8, 2024
SECOND SUNDAY OF ADVENT

First Reading: Baruch 5: 1-9

Responsorial Psalm: Psalms 126: 1-2, 2-3, 4-5, 6

Second Reading: Philippians 1: 4-6, 8-11

Alleluia: Luke 3: 4, 6

Gospel: Luke 3: 1-6

––––––––––––––––

First Reading: Baruch 5: 1-9

1 Put off, O Jerusalem, the garment of thy mourning, and affliction: and put on the beauty, and honour of that everlasting glory which thou hast from God.

2 God will clothe thee with the double garment of justice, and will set a crown on thy head of everlasting honour.

3 For God will shew his brightness in thee, to every one under heaven.

4 For thy name shall be named to thee by God for ever: the peace of justice, and honour of piety.

5 Arise, O Jerusalem, and stand on high: and look about towards the east, and behold thy children gathered together from the rising to the setting sun, by the word of the Holy One rejoicing in the remembrance of God.

6 For they went out from thee on foot, led by the enemies: but the Lord will bring them to thee exalted with honour as children of the kingdom.

7 For God hath appointed to bring down every high mountain, and the everlasting rocks, and to fill up the valleys to make them even with the ground: that Israel may walk diligently to the honour of God.

8 Moreover the woods, and every sweet-smelling tree have overshadowed Israel by the commandment of God.

9 For God will bring Israel with joy in the light of his majesty, with mercy, and justice, that cometh from him.

Responsorial Psalm: Psalms 126: 1-2, 2-3, 4-5, 6

R. (3) The Lord has done great things for us; we are filled with joy.

1 When the lord brought back the captivity of Sion, we became like men comforted.

2ab Then was our mouth filled with gladness; and our tongue with joy.

R. The Lord has done great things for us; we are filled with joy.

2cd Then shall they say among the Gentiles: The Lord hath done great things for them.

3 The Lord hath done great things for us: we are become joyful.

R. The Lord has done great things for us; we are filled with joy.

4 Turn again our captivity, O Lord, as a stream in the south.

5 They that sow in tears shall reap in joy.

R. The Lord has done great things for us; we are filled with joy.

6 Going they went and wept, casting their seeds. But coming they shall come with joyfulness, carrying their sheaves.

R. The Lord has done great things for us; we are filled with joy.

Second Reading: Philippians 1: 4-6, 8-11

4 Always in all my prayers making supplication for you all, with joy;

5 For your communication in the gospel of Christ from the first day until now.

6 Being confident of this very thing, that he, who hath begun a good work in you, will perfect it unto the day of Christ Jesus.

8 For God is my witness, how I long after you all in the bowels of Jesus Christ.

9 And this I pray, that your charity may more and more abound in knowledge, and in all understanding:

10 That you may approve the better things, that you may be sincere and without offence unto the day of Christ,

11 Filled with the fruit of justice, through Jesus Christ, unto the glory and praise of God.

Alleluia: Luke 3: 4, 6

R. Alleluia, alleluia.

4, 6 Prepare the way of the Lord, make straight his paths: all flesh shall see the salvation of God.

R. Alleluia, alleluia.

Gospel: Luke 3: 1-6

1 Now in the fifteenth year of the reign of Tiberius Caesar, Pontius Pilate being governor of Judea, and Herod being tetrarch of Galilee, and Philip his brother tetrarch of Iturea, and the country of Trachonitis, and Lysanias tetrarch of Abilina;

2 Under the high priests Annas and Caiphas; the word of the Lord was made unto John, the son of Zachary, in the desert.

3 And he came into all the country about the Jordan, preaching the baptism of penance for the remission of sins;

4 As it was written in the book of the sayings of Isaias the prophet: A voice of one crying in the wilderness: Prepare ye the way of the Lord, make straight his paths.

5 Every valley shall be filled; and every mountain and hill shall be brought low; and the crooked shall be made straight; and the rough ways plain;

6 And all flesh shall see the salvation of God.

~

MONDAY DECEMBER 9, 2024

First Reading: Genesis 3: 9-15, 20

Responsorial Psalm: Psalms 98: 1, 2-3ab, 3cd-4

Second Reading: Ephesians 1: 3-6, 11-12

Alleluia: Luke 1: 28

Gospel: Luke 1: 26-38

First Reading: Genesis 3: 9-15, 20

9 And the Lord God called Adam, and said to him: Where art thou?

10 And he said: I heard thy voice in paradise; and I was afraid, because I was naked, and I hid myself.

11 And he said to him: And who hath told thee that thou wast naked, but that thou hast eaten of the tree whereof I commanded thee that thou shouldst not eat?

12 And Adam said: The woman, whom thou gavest me to be my companion, gave me of the tree, and I did eat.

13 And the Lord God said to the woman: Why hast thou done this? And she answered: The serpent deceived me, and I did eat.

14 And the Lord God said to the serpent: Because thou hast done this thing, thou art cursed among all cattle, and beasts of the earth: upon thy breast shalt thou go, and earth shalt thou eat all the days of thy life.

15 I will put enmities between thee and the woman, and thy seed and her seed: she shall crush thy head, and thou shalt lie in wait for her heel.

20 And Adam called the name of his wife Eve: because she was the mother of all the living.

Responsorial Psalm: Psalms 98: 1, 2-3ab, 3cd-4

R. (1) Sing to the Lord a new song, for he has done marvelous deeds.

1 Sing ye to the Lord anew canticle: because he hath done wonderful things. His right hand hath wrought for him salvation, and his arm is holy.

R. Sing to the Lord a new song, for he has done marvelous deeds.

2 The Lord hath made known his salvation: he hath revealed his justice in the sight of the Gentiles.

3ab He hath remembered his mercy his truth toward the house of Israel.

R. Sing to the Lord a new song, for he has done marvelous deeds.

3cd All the ends of the earth have seen the salvation of our God.

4 Sing joyfully to God, all the earth; make melody, rejoice and sing.

R. Sing to the Lord a new song, for he has done marvelous deeds.

Second Reading: Ephesians 1: 3-6, 11-12

3 Blessed be the God and Father of our Lord Jesus Christ, who hath blessed us with spiritual blessings in heavenly places, in Christ:

4 As he chose us in him before the foundation of the world, that we should be holy and unspotted in his sight in charity.

5 Who hath predestinated us unto the adoption of children through Jesus Christ unto himself: according to the purpose of his will:

6 Unto the praise of the glory of his grace, in which he hath graced us in his beloved son.

11 In whom we also are called by lot, being predestinated according to the purpose of him who worketh all things according to the counsel of his will.

12 That we may be unto the praise of his glory, we who before hoped Christ:

Alleluia: Luke 1: 28

R. Alleluia, alleluia.

28 Hail, Mary, full of grace, the Lord is with you; blessed are you among women.

R. Alleluia, alleluia.

Gospel: Luke 1: 26-38

26 And in the sixth month, the angel Gabriel was sent from God into a city of Galilee, called Nazareth,

27 To a virgin espoused to a man whose name was Joseph, of the house of David; and the virgin's name was Mary.

28 And the angel being come in, said unto her: Hail, full of grace, the Lord is with thee: blessed art thou among women.

29 Who having heard, was troubled at his saying, and thought with herself what manner of salutation this should be.

30 And the angel said to her: Fear not, Mary, for thou hast found grace with God.

31 Behold thou shalt conceive in thy womb, and shalt bring forth a son; and thou shalt call his name Jesus.

32 He shall be great, and shall be called the Son of the most High; and the Lord God shall give unto him the throne of David his father; and he shall reign in the house of Jacob for ever.

33 And of his kingdom there shall be no end.

34 And Mary said to the angel: How shall this be done, because I know not man?

35 And the angel answering, said to her: The Holy Ghost shall come upon thee, and the power of the most High shall overshadow thee. And therefore also the Holy which shall be born of thee shall be called the Son of God.

36 And behold thy cousin Elizabeth, she also hath conceived a son in her old age; and this is the sixth month with her that is called barren:

37 Because no word shall be impossible with God.

38 And Mary said: Behold the handmaid of the Lord; be it done to me according to thy word. And the angel departed from her.

∿

TUESDAY DECEMBER 10, 2024

First Reading: Isaiah 40: 1-11

Responsorial Psalm: Psalms 96: 1-2, 3 and 10ac, 11-12, 13

Gospel: Matthew 18: 12-14

First Reading: Isaiah 40: 1-11

1 Be comforted, be comforted, my people, saith your God.

2 Speak ye to the heart of Jerusalem, and call to her: for her evil is come to an end, her iniquity is forgiven: she hath received of the hand of the Lord double for all her sins.

3 The voice of one crying in the desert: Prepare ye the way of the Lord, make straight in the wilderness the paths of our God.

4 Every valley shall be exalted, and every mountain and hill shall be made low, and the crooked shall become straight, and the rough ways plain.

5 And the glory of the Lord shall be revealed, and all flesh together shall see, that the mouth of the Lord hath spoken.

6 The voice of one, saying: Cry. And I said: What shall I cry? All flesh is grass, and all the glory thereof as the flower of the held.

7 The grass is withered, and the dower is fallen, because the spirit of the Lord hath blown upon it. Indeed the people is grass:

8 The grass is withered, and the flower is fallen: but the word of our Lord endureth for ever.

9 Get thee up upon a high mountain, thou that bringest good tidings to Sion: lift up thy voice with strength, thou that bringest good tidings to Jerusalem: lift it up, fear not. Say to the cities of Juda: Behold your God:

10 Behold the Lord God shall come with strength, and his arm shall rule: Behold his reward is with him and his work is before him.

11 He shall feed his flock like a shepherd: he shall gather together the lambs with his arm, and shall take them up in his bosom, and he himself shall carry them that are with young.

Responsorial Psalm: Psalms 96: 1-2, 3 and 10ac, 11-12, 13

R. (Isaiah 40:10ab) The Lord our God comes with power.

1 Sing ye to the Lord a new canticle: sing to the Lord, all the earth.

2 Sing ye to the Lord and bless his name: shew forth his salvation from day to day.

R. The Lord our God comes with power.

3 Declare his glory among the Gentiles: his wonders among all people.

10 Say ye among the Gentiles, the Lord hath reigned. he will judge the people with justice.

R. The Lord our God comes with power.

11 Let the heavens rejoice, and let the earth be glad, let the sea be moved, and the fulness thereof:

12 The fields and all things that are in them shall be joyful. Then shall all the trees of the woods rejoice

R. The Lord our God comes with power.

13 Before the face of the Lord, because he cometh: because he cometh to judge the earth. He shall judge the world with justice, and the people with his truth.

R. The Lord our God comes with power.

Alleluia

R. Alleluia, alleluia.

The day of the Lord is near; Behold, he comes to save us.

R. Alleluia, alleluia.

Gospel: Matthew 18: 12-14

12 What think you? If a man have an hundred sheep, and one of them should go astray: doth he not leave the ninety-nine in the mountains, and go to seek that which is gone astray?

13 And if it so be that he find it: Amen I say to you, he rejoiceth more for that, than for the ninety-nine that went not astray.

14 Even so it is not the will of your Father, who is in heaven, that one of these little ones should perish.

~

WEDNESDAY DECEMBER 11, 2024

First Reading: Isaiah 40: 25-31

Responsorial Psalm: Psalms 103: 1-2, 3-4, 8 and 10

Gospel: Matthew 11: 28-30

First Reading: Isaiah 40: 25-31

25 And to whom have ye likened me, or made me equal, saith the Holy One?

26 Lift up your eyes on high, and see who hath created these things: who bringeth out their host by number, and calleth them all by their names: by the greatness of his might, and strength, and power, not one of them was missing.

27 Why sayest thou, O Jacob, and speakest, O Israel: My way is hid from the Lord, and my judgment is passed over from my God?

28 Knowest thou not, or hast thou not heard? the Lord is the everlasting God, who hath created the ends of the earth: he shall not faint, nor labour, neither is there any searching out of his wisdom.

29 It is he that giveth strength to the weary, and increaseth force and might to them that are not.

30 Youths shall faint, and labour, and young men shall fall by infirmity.

31 But they that hope in the Lord shall renew their strength, they shall take wings as eagles, they shall run and not be weary, they shall walk and not faint.

Responsorial Psalm: Psalms 103: 1-2, 3-4, 8 and 10

R. (1) O bless the Lord, my soul!

1 Bless the Lord, O my soul: and let all that is within me bless his holy name.

2 Bless the Lord, O my soul, and never forget all he hath done for thee.

R. O bless the Lord, my soul!

3 Who forgiveth all thy iniquities: who healeth all thy diseases.

4 Who redeemeth thy life from destruction: who crowneth thee with mercy and compassion.

R. O bless the Lord, my soul!

8 The Lord is compassionate and merciful: longsuffering and plenteous in mercy.

10 He hath not dealt with us according to our sins: nor rewarded us according to our iniquities.

R. O bless the Lord, my soul!

Alleluia

R. Alleluia, alleluia.

Behold, the Lord comes to save his people; blessed are those prepared to meet him.

R. Alleluia, alleluia.

Gospel: Matthew 11: 28-30

28 Come to me, all you that labour, and are burdened, and I will refresh you.

29 Take up my yoke upon you, and learn of me, because I am meek, and humble of heart: and you shall find rest to your souls.

30 For my yoke is sweet and my burden light.

∼

First Reading: Zechariah 2: 14-17 or Revelation 11: 19a; 12: 1-6a, 10ab

Responsorial Psalm: Judith 13: 18bcde, 19

Gospel: Luke 1: 26-38 or Luke 1: 39-47

First Reading: Zechariah 2: 14-17 or Revelation 11: 19a; 12: 1-6a, 10ab

14 Sing praise, and rejoice, O daughter of Sion: for behold I come, and I will dwell in the midst of thee: saith the Lord.

15 And many nations shall be joined to the Lord in that day, and they shall be my people, and I will dwell in the midst of thee: and thou shalt know that the Lord of hosts hath sent me to thee.

16 And the Lord shall possess Juda his portion in the sanctified land: and he shall yet choose Jerusalem.

17 Let all flesh be silent at the presence of the Lord: for he is risen up out of his. holy habitation.

Or

19a And the temple of God was opened in heaven: and the ark of his testament was seen in his temple

1 And a great sign appeared in heaven: A woman clothed with the sun, and the moon under her feet, and on her head a crown of twelve stars:

2 And being with child, she cried travailing in birth, and was in pain to be delivered.

3 And there was seen another sign in heaven: and behold a great red dragon, having seven heads, and ten horns: and on his head seven diadems:

4 And his tail drew the third part of the stars of heaven, and cast them to the earth: and the dragon stood before the woman who was ready to be delivered; that, when she should be delivered, he might devour her son.

5 And she brought forth a man child, who was to rule all nations with an iron rod: and her son was taken up to God, and to his throne.

6a And the woman fled into the wilderness, where she had a place prepared by God.

10ab And I heard a loud voice in heaven, saying: Now is come salvation, and strength, and the kingdom of our God, and the power of his Christ.

Responsorial Psalm: Judith 13: 18bcde, 19

R. (15:9d) You are the highest honor of our race.

18bcde Blessed art thou, O daughter, by the Lord the most high God, above all women upon the earth. Blessed be the Lord who made heaven and earth.

R. You are the highest honor of our race.

19 And all the people said: So be it, so be it. And Achior being called for came, and Judith said to him: The God of Israel, to whom thou gavest testimony, that he revengeth himself of his enemies, he hath cut off the head of all the unbelievers this night by my hand.

R. You are the highest honor of our race.

Alleluia

R. Alleluia, alleluia.

Blessed are you, holy Virgin Mary, deserving of all praise; from you rose the sun of justice, Christ our God.

R. Alleluia, alleluia.

Gospel: Luke 1: 26-38 or Luke 1: 39-47

26 And in the sixth month, the angel Gabriel was sent from God into a city of Galilee, called Nazareth,

27 To a virgin espoused to a man whose name was Joseph, of the house of David; and the virgin's name was Mary.

28 And the angel being come in, said unto her: Hail, full of grace, the Lord is with thee: blessed art thou among women.

29 Who having heard, was troubled at his saying, and thought with herself what manner of salutation this should be.

30 And the angel said to her: Fear not, Mary, for thou hast found grace with God.

31 Behold thou shalt conceive in thy womb, and shalt bring forth a son; and thou shalt call his name Jesus.

32 He shall be great, and shall be called the Son of the most High; and the Lord God shall give unto him the throne of David his father; and he shall reign in the house of Jacob for ever.

33 And of his kingdom there shall be no end.

34 And Mary said to the angel: How shall this be done, because I know not man?

35 And the angel answering, said to her: The Holy Ghost shall come upon thee, and the power of the most High shall overshadow thee. And therefore also the Holy which shall be born of thee shall be called the Son of God.

36 And behold thy cousin Elizabeth, she also hath conceived a son in her old age; and this is the sixth month with her that is called barren:

37 Because no word shall be impossible with God.

38 And Mary said: Behold the handmaid of the Lord; be it done to me according to thy word. And the angel departed from her.

Or

39 And Mary rising up in those days, went into the hill country with haste into a city of Juda.

40 And she entered into the house of Zachary, and saluted Elizabeth.

41 And it came to pass, that when Elizabeth heard the salutation of Mary, the infant leaped in her womb. And Elizabeth was filled with the Holy Ghost:

42 And she cried out with a loud voice, and said: Blessed art thou among women, and blessed is the fruit of thy womb.

43 And whence is this to me, that the mother of my Lord should come to me?

44 For behold as soon as the voice of thy salutation sounded in my ears, the infant in my womb leaped for joy.

45 And blessed art thou that hast believed, because those things shall be accomplished that were spoken to thee by the Lord.

46 And Mary said: My soul doth magnify the Lord.

47 And my spirit hath rejoiced in God my Saviour.

~

FRIDAY DECEMBER 13, 2024

First Reading: Isaiah 48: 17-19

Responsorial Psalm: Psalms 1: 1-2, 3, 4 and 6

Gospel: Matthew 11: 16-19

First Reading: Isaiah 48: 17-19

17 Thus saith the Lord thy redeemer, the Holy One of Israel: I am the Lord thy God that teach thee profitable things, that govern thee in the way that thou walkest.

18 O that thou hadst hearkened to my commandments: thy peace had been as a river, and thy justice as the waves of the sea,

19 And thy seed had been as the sand, and the offspring of thy bowels like the gravel thereof: his name should not have perished, nor have been destroyed from before my face.

Responsorial Psalm: Psalms 1: 1-2, 3, 4 and 6

R. (John 8:12) Those who follow you, Lord, will have the light of life.

1 Blessed is the man who hath not walked in the counsel of the ungodly, nor stood in the way of sinners, nor sat in the chair of pestilence.

2 But his will is in the law of the Lord, and on his law he shall meditate day and night.

R. Those who follow you, Lord, will have the light of life.

3 And he shall be like a tree which is planted near the running waters, which shall bring forth its fruit, in due season. And his leaf shall not fall off: and all whatsoever he shall do shall prosper.

R. Those who follow you, Lord, will have the light of life.

4 Not so the wicked, not so: but like the dust, which the wind driveth from the face of the earth.

6 For the Lord knoweth the way of the just: and the way of the wicked shall perish.

R. Those who follow you, Lord, will have the light of life.

Alleluia

R. Alleluia, alleluia.

The Lord will come; go out to meet him! He is the prince of peace.

R. Alleluia, alleluia.

Gospel: Matthew 11: 16-19

16 But whereunto shall I esteem this generation to be like? It is like to children sitting in the market place.

17 Who crying to their companions say: We have piped to you, and you have not danced: we have lamented, and you have not mourned.

18 For John came neither eating nor drinking; and they say: He hath a devil.

19 The Son of man came eating and drinking, and they say: Behold a man that is a glutton and a wine drinker, a friend of publicans and sinners. And wisdom is justified by her children.

～

SATURDAY DECEMBER 14, 2024

First Reading: Sirach 48: 1-4, 9-11

Responsorial Psalm: Psalms 80: 2ac and 3b, 15-16, 18-19

Alleluia: Luke 3: 4, 6

Gospel: Matthew 17: 9a, 10-13

―――――――――

First Reading: Sirach 48: 1-4, 9-11

1 And Elias the prophet stood up, as a fire, and his word burnt like a torch.

2 He brought a famine upon them, and they that provoked him in their envy, were reduced to a small number, for they could not endure the commandments of the Lord.

3 By the word of the Lord he shut up the heaven, and he brought down fire from heaven thrice.

4 Thus was Elias magnified in his wondrous works. And who can glory like to thee?

9 Who wast taken up in a whirlwind of fire, in a chariot of fiery horses.

10 Who art registered in the judgments of times to appease the wrath of the Lord, to reconcile the heart of the father to the son, and to restore the tribes of Jacob.

11 Blessed are they that saw thee, and were honoured with thy friendship.

Responsorial Psalm: Psalms 80: 2ac and 3b, 15-16, 18-19

R. (4) Lord, make us turn to you; let us see your face and we shall be saved.

2ac Give ear, O thou that rulest Israel: Thou that sittest upon the cherubims, shine forth

3b Stir up thy might.

R. Lord, make us turn to you; let us see your face and we shall be saved.

15 Turn again, O God of hosts, look down from heaven, and see, and visit this vineyard:

16 And perfect the same which thy right hand hath planted: and upon the son of man whom thou hast confirmed for thyself.

R. Lord, make us turn to you; let us see your face and we shall be saved.

18 Let thy hand be upon the man of thy right hand: and upon the son of man whom thou hast confirmed for thyself.

19 And we depart not from thee, thou shalt quicken us: and we will call upon thy name.

R. Lord, make us turn to you; let us see your face and we shall be saved.

Alleluia: Luke 3: 4, 6

R. Alleluia, alleluia.

4, 6 Prepare the way of the Lord, make straight his paths: All flesh shall see the salvation of God.

R. Alleluia, alleluia.

Gospel: Matthew 17: 9a, 10-13

9 And as they came down from the mountain, Jesus charged them, saying: Tell the vision to no man, till the Son of man be risen from the dead.

10 And his disciples asked him, saying: Why then do the scribes say that Elias must come first?

11 But he answering, said to them: Elias indeed shall come, and restore all things.

12 But I say to you, that Elias is already come, and they knew him not, but have done unto him whatsoever they had a mind. So also the Son of man shall suffer from them.

13 Then the disciples understood, that he had spoken to them of John the Baptist.

～

SUNDAY DECEMBER 15, 2024
THIRD SUNDAY OF ADVENT

First Reading: Zephaniah 3: 14-18a

Responsorial Psalm: Isaiah 12: 2-3, 4, 5-6

Second Reading: Philippians 4: 4-7

Alleluia: Isaiah 61: 1

Gospel: Luke 3: 10-18

First Reading: Zephaniah 3: 14-18a

14 Give praise, O daughter of Sion: shout, O Israel: be glad, and rejoice with all thy heart, O daughter of Jerusalem.

15 The Lord hath taken away thy judgment, he hath turned away thy enemies: the king of Israel the Lord is in the midst of thee, thou shalt fear evil no more.

16 In that day it shall be said to Jerusalem: Fear not: to Sion: Let not thy hands be weakened.

17 The Lord thy God in the midst of thee is mighty, he will save: he will rejoice over thee with gladness, he will be silent in his love, he will be joyful over thee in praise.

18a The triflers that were departed from the law, I will gather together.

Responsorial Psalm: Isaiah 12: 2-3, 4, 5-6

R. (6) Cry out with joy and gladness: for among you is the great and Holy One of Israel.

2 Behold, God is my saviour, I will deal confidently, and will not fear: O because the Lord is my strength, and my praise, and he is become my salvation.

3 You shall draw waters with joy out of the saviour's fountains:

R. Cry out with joy and gladness: for among you is the great and Holy One of Israel.

4 And you shall say in that day: Praise ye the Lord, and call upon his name: make his works known among the people: remember that his name is high.

R. Cry out with joy and gladness: for among you is the great and Holy One of Israel.

5 Sing ye to the Lord, for he hath done great things: shew this forth in all the earth.

6 Rejoice, and praise, O thou habitation of Sion: for great is he that is in the midst of thee, the Holy One of Israel.

R. Cry out with joy and gladness: for among you is the great and Holy One of Israel.

Second Reading: Philippians 4: 4-7

4 Rejoice in the Lord always; again, I say, rejoice.

5 Let your modesty be known to all men. The Lord is nigh.

6 Be nothing solicitous; but in every thing, by prayer and supplication, with thanksgiving, let your petitions be made known to God.

7 And the peace of God, which surpasseth all understanding, keep your hearts and minds in Christ Jesus.

Alleluia: Isaiah 61: 1

R. Alleluia, alleluia.

1 The Spirit of the Lord is upon me, because he has anointed me to bring glad tidings to the poor.

R. Alleluia, alleluia.

Gospel: Luke 3: 10-18

10 And the people asked him, saying: What then shall we do?

11 And he answering, said to them: He that hath two coats, let him give to him that hath none; and he that hath meat, let him do in like manner.

12 And the publicans also came to be baptized, and said to him: Master, what shall we do?

13 But he said to them: Do nothing more than that which is appointed you.

14 And the soldiers also asked him, saying: And what shall we do? And he said to them: Do violence to no man; neither calumniate any man; and be content with your pay.

15 And as the people were of opinion, and all were thinking in their hearts of John, that perhaps he might be the Christ;

16 John answered, saying unto all: I indeed baptize you with water; but there shall come one mightier than I, the latchet of whose shoes I am not worthy to loose: he shall baptize you with the Holy Ghost, and with fire:

17 Whose fan is in his hand, and he will purge his floor, and will gather the wheat into his barn; but the chaff he will burn with unquenchable fire.

18 And many other things exhorting, did he preach to the people.

~

MONDAY DECEMBER 16, 2024

First Reading: Numbers 24: 2-7, 15-17

Responsorial Psalm: Psalms 25: 4-5ab, 6 and 7bc, 8-9

Alleluia: Psalms 85: 8

Gospel: Matthew 21: 23-27

First Reading: Numbers 24: 2-7, 15-17

2 And lifting up his eyes, he saw Israel abiding in their tents by their tribes: and the spirit of God rushing upon him,

3 He took up his parable and said: Balaam the son of Beor hath said: The man hath said, whose eye ire stopped up:

4 The hearer of the words of God hath said, he that hath beheld the vision of the Almighty, he that falleth, and so his eyes are opened:

5 How beautiful are thy tabernacles, O Jacob, and thy tents, O Israel!

6 As woody valleys, as watered gardens near the rivers, as tabernacles which the Lord hath pitched, as cedars by the waterside.

7 Water shall flow out of his bucket, and his seed shall be in many waters. For Agag his king shall be removed, and his kingdom shall be taken awry.

15 Therefore taking up his parable, again he said: Balaam the son of Beor hath said: The man whose eye is stopped up, hath said:

16 The hearer of the words of God hath said, who knoweth the doctrine of the Highest, and seeth the visions of the Almighty, who falling hath his eyes opened:

17 I shall see him, but not now: I shall behold him, but not near. A STAR SHALL RISE out of Jacob and a sceptre shall spring up from Israel.

Responsorial Psalm: Psalms 25: 4-5ab, 6 and 7bc, 8-9

R. (4) Teach me your ways, O Lord.

4 Let all them be confounded that act unjust things without cause. shew, O Lord, thy ways to me, and teach me thy paths.

5ab Direct me in thy truth, and teach me; for thou art God my Saviour.

R. Teach me your ways, O Lord.

6 Remember, O Lord, thy bowels of compassion; and thy mercies that are from the beginning of the world.

7bc According to thy mercy remember thou me: for thy goodness' sake, O Lord.

R. Teach me your ways, O Lord.

8 The Lord is sweet and righteous: therefore he will give a law to sinners in the way.

9 He will guide the mild in judgment: he will teach the meek his ways.

R. Teach me your ways, O Lord.

Alleluia: Psalms 85: 8

R. Alleluia, alleluia.

8 Show us, LORD, your love, and grant us your salvation.

R. Alleluia, alleluia.

Gospel: Matthew 21: 23-27

23 And when he was come into the temple, there came to him, as he was teaching, the chief priests and ancients of the people, saying: By what authority dost thou these things? and who hath given thee this authority?

24 Jesus answering, said to them: I also will ask you one word, which if you shall tell me, I will also tell you by what authority I do these things.

25 The baptism of John, whence was it? from heaven or from men? But they thought within themselves, saying:

26 If we shall say, from heaven, he will say to us: Why then did you not believe him? But if we shall say, from men, we are afraid of the multitude: for all held John as a prophet.

27 And answering Jesus, they said: We know not. He also said to them: Neither do I tell you by what authority I do these things.

First Reading: Genesis 49: 2, 8-10

Responsorial Psalm: Psalms 72: 1-2, 3-4ab, 7-8, 17

Gospel: Matthew 1: 1-17

First Reading: Genesis 49: 2, 8-10

2 Gather yourselves together, and hear, O ye sons of Jacob, hearken to Israel your father:

8 Juda, thee shall thy brethren praise: thy hands shall be on the necks of thy enemies: the sons of thy father shall bow down to thee.

9 Juda is a lion's whelp: to the prey, my son, thou art gone up: resting thou hast couched as a lion, and as a lioness, who shall rouse him?

10 The sceptre shall not be taken away from Juda, nor a ruler from his thigh, till he come that is to be sent, and he shall be the expectation of nations.

Responsorial Psalm: Psalms 72: 1-2, 3-4ab, 7-8, 17

R. (7) Justice shall flourish in his time, and fullness of peace for ever.

1, 2 Give to the king thy judgment, O God: and to the king's son thy justice: To judge thy people with justice, and thy poor with judgment.

R. Justice shall flourish in his time, and fullness of peace for ever.

3 Let the mountains receive peace for the people: and the hills justice.

4ab He shall judge the poor of the people, and he shall save the children of the poor.

R. Justice shall flourish in his time, and fullness of peace for ever.

7 In his days shall justice spring up, and abundance of peace, till the moon be taken sway.

8 And he shall rule from sea to sea, and from the river unto the ends of the earth.

R. Justice shall flourish in his time, and fullness of peace for ever.

17 Let his name be blessed for evermore: his name continueth before the sun. And in him shall all the tribes of the earth be blessed: all nations shall magnify him.

R. Justice shall flourish in his time, and fullness of peace for ever.

Alleluia

R. Alleluia, alleluia.

O Wisdom of our God Most High, guiding creation with power and love: come to teach us the path of knowledge!

R. Alleluia, alleluia.

Gospel: Matthew 1: 1-17

1 The book of the generation of Jesus Christ, the son of David, the son of Abraham:

2 Abraham begot Isaac. And Isaac begot Jacob. And Jacob begot Judas and his brethren.

3 And Judas begot Phares and Zara of Thamar. And Phares begot Esron. And Esron begot Aram.

4 And Aram begot Aminadab. And Aminadab begot Naasson. And Naasson begot Salmon.

5 And Salmon begot Booz of Rahab. And Booz begot Obed of Ruth. And Obed begot Jesse.

6 And Jesse begot David the king. And David the king begot Solomon, of her that had been the wife of Urias.

7 And Solomon begot Roboam. And Roboam begot Abia. And Abia begot Asa.

8 And Asa begot Josaphat. And Josaphat begot Joram. And Joram begot Ozias.

9 And Ozias begot Joatham. And Joatham begot Achaz. And Achaz begot Ezechias.

10 And Ezechias begot Manasses. And Manasses begot Amon. And Amon begot Josias.

11 And Josias begot Jechonias and his brethren in the transmigration of Babylon.

12 And after the transmigration of Babylon, Jechonias begot Salathiel. And Salathiel begot Zorobabel.

13 And Zorobabel begot Abiud. And Abiud begot Eliacim. And Eliacim begot Azor.

14 And Azor begot Sadoc. And Sadoc begot Achim. And Achim begot Eliud.

15 And Eliud begot Eleazar. And Eleazar begot Mathan. And Mathan begot Jacob.

16 And Jacob begot Joseph the husband of Mary, of whom was born Jesus, who is called Christ.

17 So all the generations, from Abraham to David, are fourteen generations. And from David to the transmigration of Babylon, are fourteen generations: and from the transmigration of Babylon to Christ are fourteen generations.

$\sim$

WEDNESDAY DECEMBER 18, 2024

First Reading: Jeremiah 23: 5-8

Responsorial Psalm: Psalms 72: 1-2, 12-13, 18-19

Gospel: Matthew 1: 18-25

First Reading: Jeremiah 23: 5-8

5 Behold the days come, saith the Lord, and I will raise up to David a just branch: and a king shall reign, and shall be wise, and shall execute judgement and justice in the earth.

6 In those days shall Juda be saved, and Israel shall dwell confidently: and this is the name that they shall call him: the Lord our just one.

7 Therefore behold the days to come, saith the Lord, and they shall say no more: The Lord liveth, who brought up the children of Israel out of the land of Egypt:

8 But the Lord liveth, who hath brought out, and brought hither the seed of

the house of Israel from the land of the north, and out of all the lands, to which I had cast them forth: and they shall dwell in their own land.

Responsorial Psalm: Psalms 72: 1-2, 12-13, 18-19

R. (7) Justice shall flourish in his time, and fullness of peace for ever.

1, 2 Give to the king thy judgment, O God: and to the king's son thy justice: To judge thy people with justice, and thy poor with judgment.

R. Justice shall flourish in his time, and fullness of peace for ever.

12 For he shall deliver the poor from the mighty: and the needy that had no helper.

13 He shall spare the poor and needy: and he shall save the souls of the poor.

R. Justice shall flourish in his time, and fullness of peace for ever.

18 Blessed be the Lord, the God of Israel, who alone doth wonderful things.

19 And blessed be the name of his majesty for ever: and the whole earth shall be filled with his majesty. So be it. So be it.

R. Justice shall flourish in his time, and fullness of peace for ever.

Alleluia

R. Alleluia, alleluia.

O Leader of the House of Israel, giver of the Law to Moses on Sinai: come to rescue us with your mighty power!

R. Alleluia, alleluia.

Gospel: Matthew 1: 18-25

18 Now the generation of Christ was in this wise. When as his mother Mary was espoused to Joseph, before they came together, she was found with child, of the Holy Ghost.

19 Whereupon Joseph her husband, being a just man, and not willing publicly to expose her, was minded to put her away privately.

20 But while he thought on these things, behold the angel of the Lord appeared to him in his sleep, saying: Joseph, son of David, fear not to take unto thee Mary thy wife, for that which is conceived in her, is of the Holy Ghost.

21 And she shall bring forth a son: and thou shalt call his name JESUS. For he shall save his people from their sins.

22 Now all this was done that it might be fulfilled which the Lord spoke by the prophet, saying:

23 Behold a virgin shall be with child, and bring forth a son, and they shall call his name Emmanuel, which being interpreted is, God with us.

24 And Joseph rising up from sleep, did as the angel of the Lord had commanded him, and took unto him his wife.

25 And he knew her not till she brought forth her firstborn son: and he called his name JESUS.

～

THURSDAY DECEMBER 19, 2024

First Reading: Judges 13: 2-7, 24-25a

Responsorial Psalm: Psalms 71: 3-4a, 5-6ab, 16-17

Gospel: Luke 1: 5-25

First Reading: Judges 13: 2-7, 24-25a

2 Now there was a certain man of Saraa, and of the race of Dan, whose name was Manue, and his wife was barren.

3 And an angel of the Lord appeared to her, and said: Thou art barren and without children: but thou shalt conceive and bear a son.

4 Now therefore beware and drink no wine nor strong drink, and eat not any unclean thing.

5 Because thou shalt conceive and bear a son, and no razor shall touch his head: for he shall be a Nazarite of God, from his infancy, and from his mother's womb, and he shall begin to deliver Israel from the hands of the Philistines.

6 And when she was come to her husband she said to him: A man of God came to me, having the countenance of an angel, very awful. And when I asked him who he was, and whence he came, and by what name he was called, he would not tell me.

7 But he answered thus: Behold thou shalt conceive and bear a son: beware thou drink no wine, nor strong drink, nor eat any unclean thing: for the child shall be a Nazarite of God from his infancy, from his mother's womb until the day of his death.

24 And she bore a son, and called his name Samson. And the child grew, and the Lord blessed him.

25a And the spirit of the Lord began to be with him.

Responsorial Psalm: Psalms 71: 3-4a, 5-6ab, 16-17

R. (8) My mouth shall be filled with your praise, and I will sing your glory!

3 Be thou unto me a God, a protector, and a place of strength: that thou mayst make me safe. For thou art my firmament and my refuge.

4a Deliver me, O my God, out of the hand of the sinner.

R. My mouth shall be filled with your praise, and I will sing your glory!

5 For thou art my patience, O Lord: my hope, O Lord, from my youth;

6ab By thee have I been confirmed from the womb: from my mother's womb thou art my protector.

R My mouth shall be filled with your praise, and I will sing your glory!

16 I will enter into the powers of the Lord: O Lord, I will be mindful of thy justice alone.

17 Thou hast taught me, O God, from my youth: and till now I will declare thy wonderful works.

R. My mouth shall be filled with your praise, and I will sing your glory!

Alleluia

R. Alleluia, alleluia.

O Root of Jesse's stem, sign of God's love for all his people: come to save us without delay!

R. Alleluia, alleluia.

Gospel: Luke 1: 5-25

5 There was in the days of Herod, the king of Judea, a certain priest named Zachary, of the course of Abia; and his wife was of the daughters of Aaron, and her name Elizabeth.

6 And they were both just before God, walking in all the commandments and justifications of the Lord without blame.

7 And they had no son, for that Elizabeth was barren, and they both were well advanced in years.

8 And it came to pass, when he executed the priestly function in the order of his course before God,

9 According to the custom of the priestly office, it was his lot to offer incense, going into the temple of the Lord.

10 And all the multitude of the people was praying without, at the hour of incense.

11 And there appeared to him an angel of the Lord, standing on the right side of the alter of incense.

12 And Zachary seeing him, was troubled, and fear fell upon him.

13 But the angel said to him: Fear not, Zachary, for thy prayer is heard; and thy wife Elizabeth shall bear thee a son, and thou shalt call his name John:

14 And thou shalt have joy and gladness, and many shall rejoice in his nativity.

15 For he shall be great before the Lord; and shall drink no wine nor strong drink: and he shall be filled with the Holy Ghost, even from his mother's womb.

16 And he shall convert many of the children of Israel to the Lord their God.

17 And he shall go before him in the spirit and power of Elias; that he may turn the hearts of the fathers unto the children, and the incredulous to the wisdom of the just, to prepare unto the Lord a perfect people.

18 And Zachary said to the angel: Whereby shall I know this? for I am an old man, and my wife is advanced in years.

19 And the angel answering, said to him: I am Gabriel, who stand before God: and am sent to speak to thee, and to bring thee these good tidings.

20 And behold, thou shalt be dumb, and shalt not be able to speak until the day wherein these things shall come to pass, because thou hast not believed my words, which shall be fulfilled in their time.

21 And the people were waiting for Zachary; and they wondered that he tarried so long in the temple.

22 And when he came out, he could not speak to them: and they understood that he had seen a vision in the temple. And he made signs to them, and remained dumb.

23 And it came to pass, after the days of his office were accomplished, he departed to his own house.

24 And after those days, Elizabeth his wife conceived, and hid herself five months, saying:

25 Thus hath the Lord dealt with me in the days wherein he hath had regard to take away my reproach among men.

$\sim$

FRIDAY DECEMBER 20, 2024

First Reading: Isaiah 7: 10-14

Responsorial Psalm: Psalms 24: 1-2, 3-4ab, 5-6

Gospel: Luke 1: 26-38

First Reading: Isaiah 7: 10-14

10 And the Lord spoke again to Achaz, saying:

11 Ask thee a sign of the Lord thy God either unto the depth of hell, or unto the height above.

12 And Achaz said: I will not ask, and I will not tempt the Lord.

13 And he said: Hear ye therefore, O house of David: Is it a small thing for you to be grievous to men, that you are grievous to my God also?

14 Therefore the Lord himself shall give you a sign. Behold a virgin shall conceive, and bear a son, and his name shall be called Emmanuel.

Responsorial Psalm: Psalms 24: 1-2, 3-4ab, 5-6

R. (7c and 10b) Let the Lord enter; he is the king of glory.

1 On the first day of the week, a psalm for David. The earth is the Lord's and the fulness thereof: the world, and all they that dwell therein.

2 For he hath founded it upon the seas; and hath prepared it upon the rivers.

R. Let the Lord enter; he is the king of glory.

3 Who shall ascend into the mountain of the Lord: or who shall stand in his holy place?

4 The innocent in hands, and clean of heart, who hath not taken his soul in vain.

R. Let the Lord enter; he is the king of glory.

5 He shall receive a blessing from the Lord, and mercy from God his Saviour.

6 This is the generation of them that seek him, of them that seek the face of the God of Jacob.

R. Let the Lord enter; he is the king of glory.

Alleluia

R. Alleluia, alleluia.

O Key of David, opening the gates of God's eternal Kingdom: come and free the prisoners of darkness!

R. Alleluia, alleluia.

Gospel: Luke 1: 26-38

26 And in the sixth month, the angel Gabriel was sent from God into a city of Galilee, called Nazareth,

27 To a virgin espoused to a man whose name was Joseph, of the house of David; and the virgin's name was Mary.

28 And the angel being come in, said unto her: Hail, full of grace, the Lord is with thee: blessed art thou among women.

29 Who having heard, was troubled at his saying, and thought with herself what manner of salutation this should be.

30 And the angel said to her: Fear not, Mary, for thou hast found grace with God.

31 Behold thou shalt conceive in thy womb, and shalt bring forth a son; and thou shalt call his name Jesus.

32 He shall be great, and shall be called the Son of the most High; and the Lord God shall give unto him the throne of David his father; and he shall reign in the house of Jacob for ever.

33 And of his kingdom there shall be no end.

34 And Mary said to the angel: How shall this be done, because I know not man?

35 And the angel answering, said to her: The Holy Ghost shall come upon thee, and the power of the most High shall overshadow thee. And therefore also the Holy which shall be born of thee shall be called the Son of God.

36 And behold thy cousin Elizabeth, she also hath conceived a son in her old age; and this is the sixth month with her that is called barren:

37 Because no word shall be impossible with God.

38 And Mary said: Behold the handmaid of the Lord; be it done to me according to thy word. And the angel departed from her.

~

SATURDAY DECEMBER 21, 2024

First Reading: Songs 2: 8-14 or Zephaniah 3: 14-18a

Responsorial Psalm: Psalms 33: 2-3, 11-12, 20-21

Gospel: Luke 1: 39-45

First Reading: Songs 2: 8-14 or Zephaniah 3: 14-18a

8 The voice of my beloved, behold he cometh leaping upon the mountains, skipping over the hills.

9 My beloved is like a roe, or a young hart. Behold he standeth behind our wall, looking through the windows, looking through the lattices.

10 Behold my beloved speaketh to me: Arise, make haste, my love, my dove, my beautiful one, and come.

11 For winter is now past, the rain is over and gone.

12 The flowers have appeared in our land, the time of pruning is come: the voice of the turtle is heard in our land:

13 The fig tree hath put forth her green figs: the vines in flower yield their sweet smell. Arise, my love, my beautiful one, and come:

14 My dove in the clefts of the rock, in the hollow places of the wall, shew me thy face, let thy voice sound in my ears: for thy voice is sweet, and thy face comely.

Or

14 Give praise, O daughter of Sion: shout, O Israel: be glad, and rejoice with all thy heart, O daughter of Jerusalem.

15 The Lord hath taken away thy judgment, he hath turned away thy enemies: the king of Israel the Lord is in the midst of thee, thou shalt fear evil no more.

16 In that day it shall be said to Jerusalem: Fear not: to Sion: Let not thy hands be weakened.

17, 18a The Lord thy God in the midst of thee is mighty, he will save: he will rejoice over thee with gladness, he will be silent in his love, he will be joyful over thee in praise.

Responsorial Psalm: Psalms 33: 2-3, 11-12, 20-21

R. (1a, 3a) Exult, you just, in the Lord! Sing to him a new song.

2 Give praise to the Lord on the harp; sing to him with the psaltery, the instrument of ten strings.

3 Sing to him a new canticle, sing well unto him with a loud noise.

R. Exult, you just, in the Lord! Sing to him a new song.

11 But the counsel of the Lord standeth for ever: the thoughts of his heart to all generations.

12 Blessed is the nation whose God is the Lord: the people whom he hath chosen for his inheritance.

R. Exult, you just, in the Lord! Sing to him a new song.

20 Our soul waiteth for the Lord: for he is our helper and protector.

21 For in him our heart shall rejoice: and in his holy name we have trusted.

R. Exult, you just, in the Lord! Sing to him a new song.

Alleluia

R. Alleluia, alleluia.

O Emmanuel, our King and Giver of Law: come to save us, Lord our God!

R. Alleluia, alleluia.

Gospel: Luke 1: 39-45

39 And Mary rising up in those days, went into the hill country with haste into a city of Juda.

40 And she entered into the house of Zachary, and saluted Elizabeth.

41 And it came to pass, that when Elizabeth heard the salutation of Mary, the infant leaped in her womb. And Elizabeth was filled with the Holy Ghost:

42 And she cried out with a loud voice, and said: Blessed art thou among women, and blessed is the fruit of thy womb.

43 And whence is this to me, that the mother of my Lord should come to me?

44 For behold as soon as the voice of thy salutation sounded in my ears, the infant in my womb leaped for joy.

45 And blessed art thou that hast believed, because those things shall be accomplished that were spoken to thee by the Lord.

❦

SUNDAY DECEMBER 22, 2024

First Reading: Micah 5: 1-4a

Responsorial Psalm: Psalms 80: 2-3, 15-16, 18-19

Second Reading: Hebrews 10: 5-10

Alleluia: Luke 1: 38

Gospel: Luke 1: 39-45

First Reading: Micah 5: 1-4a

1 Now shalt thou be laid waste, O daughter of the robber: they have laid siege against us, with a rod shall they strike the cheek of the judge of Israel.

2 AND THOU, BETHLEHEM Ephrata, art a little one among the thousands of Juda: out of thee shall he come forth unto me that is to be the ruler in Israel: and his going forth is from the beginning, from the days of eternity.

3 Therefore will he give them up even till the time wherein she that travaileth shall bring forth: and the remnant of his brethren shall be converted to the children of Israel.

4 And he shall stand, and feed in the strength of the Lord, in the height of the name of the Lord his God: and they shall be converted, for now shall he be magnified even to the ends of the earth.

Responsorial Psalm: Psalms 80: 2-3, 15-16, 18-19

R. (4) Lord, make us turn to you; let us see your face and we shall be saved.

2 Give ear, O thou that rulest Israel: thou that leadest Joseph like a sheep. Thou that sittest upon the cherubims, shine forth

3 Before Ephraim, Benjamin, and Manasses. Stir up thy might, and come to save us.

R. Lord, make us turn to you; let us see your face and we shall be saved.

15 Turn again, O God of hosts, look down from heaven, and see, and visit this vineyard:

16 And perfect the same which thy right hand hath planted: and upon the son of man whom thou hast confirmed for thyself.

R. Lord, make us turn to you; let us see your face and we shall be saved.

18 Let thy hand be upon the man of thy right hand: and upon the son of man whom thou hast confirmed for thyself.

19 And we depart not from thee, thou shalt quicken us: and we will call upon thy name.

R. Lord, make us turn to you; let us see your face and we shall be saved.

Second Reading: Hebrews 10: 5-10

5 Wherefore when he cometh into the world, he saith: Sacrifice and oblation thou wouldest not: but a body thou hast fitted to me:

6 Holocausts for sin did not please thee.

7 Then said I: Behold I come: in the head of the book it is written of me: that I should do thy will, O God.

8 In saying before, Sacrifices, and oblations, and holocausts for sin thou wouldest not, neither are they pleasing to thee, which are offered according to the law.

9 Then said I: Behold, I come to do thy will, O God: he taketh away the first, that he may establish that which followeth.

10 In the which will, we are sanctified by the oblation of the body of Jesus Christ once.

Alleluia: Luke 1: 38

R. Alleluia, alleluia.

38 Behold, I am the handmaid of the Lord. May it be done to me according to your word.

R. Alleluia, alleluia.

Gospel: Luke 1: 39-45

39 And Mary rising up in those days, went into the hill country with haste into a city of Juda.

40 And she entered into the house of Zachary, and saluted Elizabeth.

41 And it came to pass, that when Elizabeth heard the salutation of Mary, the infant leaped in her womb. And Elizabeth was filled with the Holy Ghost:

42 And she cried out with a loud voice, and said: Blessed art thou among women, and blessed is the fruit of thy womb.

43 And whence is this to me, that the mother of my Lord should come to me?

44 For behold as soon as the voice of thy salutation sounded in my ears, the infant in my womb leaped for joy.

45 And blessed art thou that hast believed, because those things shall be accomplished that were spoken to thee by the Lord.

∿

MONDAY DECEMBER 23, 2024

First Reading: Malachi 3: 1-4, 23-24

Responsorial Psalm: Psalms 25: 4-5ab, 8-9, 10 and 14

Gospel: Luke 1: 57-66

First Reading: Malachi 3: 1-4, 23-24

1 Behold I send my angel, and he shall prepare the way before my face. And presently the Lord, whom you seek, and the angel of the testament, whom you desire, shall come to his temple. Behold he cometh, saith the Lord of hosts.

2 And who shall be able to think of the day of his coming? and who shall stand to see him? for he is like a refining fire, and like the fuller's herb:

3 And he shall sit refining and cleansing the silver, and he shall purify the sons of Levi, and shall refine them as gold, and as silver, and they shall offer sacrifices to the Lord in justice.

4 And the sacrifice of Juda and of Jerusalem shall please the Lord, as in the days of old, and in the ancient years.

23 Behold I will send you Elias the prophet, before the coming of the great and dreadful day of the Lord.

24 And he shall turn the heart of the fathers to the children, and the heart of the children to their fathers: lest I come, and strike the earth with anathema.

Responsorial Psalm: Psalms 25: 4-5ab, 8-9, 10 and 14

R. (Luke 21:28) Lift up your heads and see; your redemption is near at hand.

4 Let all them be confounded that act unjust things without cause. shew, O Lord, thy ways to me, and teach me thy paths.

5ab Direct me in thy truth, and teach me; for thou art God my Saviour.

R. Lift up your heads and see; your redemption is near at hand.

8 The Lord is sweet and righteous: therefore he will give a law to sinners in the way.

9 He will guide the mild in judgment: he will teach the meek his ways.

R. Lift up your heads and see; your redemption is near at hand.

10 All the ways of the Lord are mercy and truth, to them that seek after his covenant and his testimonies.

14 The Lord is a firmament to them that fear him: and his covenant shall be made manifest to them.

R. Lift up your heads and see; your redemption is near at hand.

Alleluia

R. Alleluia, alleluia.

O King of all nations and keystone of the Church; come and save man, whom you formed from the dust!

R. Alleluia, alleluia.

Gospel: Luke 1: 57-66

57 Now Elizabeth's full time of being delivered was come, and she brought forth a son.

58 And her neighbours and kinsfolks heard that the Lord had shewed his great mercy towards her, and they congratulated with her.

59 And it came to pass, that on the eighth day they came to circumcise the child, and they called him by his father's name Zachary.

60 And his mother answering, said: Not so; but he shall be called John.

61 And they said to her: There is none of thy kindred that is called by this name.

62 And they made signs to his father, how he would have him called.

63 And demanding a writing table, he wrote, saying: John is his name. And they all wondered.

64 And immediately his mouth was opened, and his tongue loosed, and he spoke, blessing God.

65 And fear came upon all their neighbours; and all these things were noised abroad over all the hill country of Judea.

66 And all they that had heard them laid them up in their heart, saying: What an one, think ye, shall this child be? For the hand of the Lord was with him.

~

TUESDAY DECEMBER 24, 2024

First Reading: Second Samuel 7: 1-5, 8b-12, 14a, 16

Responsorial Psalm: Psalms 89: 2-3, 4-5, 27 and 29

Gospel: Luke 1: 67-79

First Reading: Second Samuel 7: 1-5, 8b-12, 14a, 16

1 And it came to pass when the king sat in his house, and the Lord had given him rest on every side from all his enemies,

2 He said to Nathan the prophet: Dost thou see that I dwell in a house of cedar, and the ark of God is lodged within skins?

3 And Nathan said to the king: Go, do all that is in thy heart: because the Lord is with thee.

4 But it came to pass that night, that the word of the Lord came to Nathan, saying:

5 Go, and say to my servant David: Thus saith the Lord: Shalt thou build me a house to dwell in?

8b Thus saith the Lord of hosts: I took thee out of the pastures from following the sheep to be ruler over my people Israel:

9 And I have been with thee wheresoever thou hast walked, and have slain all thy enemies from before thy face: and I have made thee a great man, like unto the name of the great ones that are on the earth.

10 And I will appoint a place for my people Israel, and I will plant them, and they shall dwell therein, and shall be disturbed no more: neither shall the children of iniquity afflict them any more as they did before,

11 From the day that I appointed judges over my people Israel: and I will give thee rest from all thy enemies. And the Lord foretelleth to thee, that the Lord will make thee a house.

12 And when thy days shall be fulfilled, and thou shalt sleep with thy fathers, I will raise up thy seed after thee, which shall proceed out of thy bowels, and I will establish his kingdom.

14a I will be to him a father, and he shall be to me a son.

16 And thy house shall be faithful, and thy kingdom for ever before thy face, and thy throne shall be firm for ever.

Responsorial Psalm: Psalms 89: 2-3, 4-5, 27 and 29

R. (2) For ever I will sing the goodness of the Lord.

2 The mercies of the Lord I will sing for ever. I will shew forth thy truth with my mouth to generation and generation.

3 For thou hast said: Mercy shall be built up for ever in the heavens: thy truth shall be prepared in them.

R. For ever I will sing the goodness of the Lord.

4 I have made a covenant with my elect: I have sworn to David my servant:

5 Thy seed will I settle for ever. And I will build up thy throne unto generation and generation.

R. For ever I will sing the goodness of the Lord.

27 He shall cry out to me: Thou art my father: my God, and the support of my salvation.

29 I will keep my mercy for him for ever: and my covenant faithful to him.

R. For ever I will sing the goodness of the Lord.

Alleluia

R. Alleluia, alleluia.

O Radiant Dawn, splendor of eternal light, sun of justice: come and shine on those who dwell in darkness and in the shadow of death.

R. Alleluia, alleluia.

Gospel: Luke 1: 67-79

67 And Zachary his father was filled with the Holy Ghost; and he prophesied, saying:

68 Blessed be the Lord God of Israel; because he hath visited and wrought the redemption of his people:

69 And hath raised up an horn of salvation to us, in the house of David his servant:

70 As he spoke by the mouth of his holy prophets, who are from the beginning:

71 Salvation from our enemies, and from the hand of all that hate us:

72 To perform mercy to our fathers, and to remember his holy testament,

73 The oath, which he swore to Abraham our father, that he would grant to us,

74 That being delivered from the hand of our enemies, we may serve him without fear,

75 In holiness and justice before him, all our days.

76 And thou, child, shalt be called the prophet of the Highest: for thou shalt go before the face of the Lord to prepare his ways:

77 To give knowledge of salvation to his people, unto the remission of their sins:

78 Through the bowels of the mercy of our God, in which the Orient from on high hath visited us:

79 To enlighten them that sit in darkness, and in the shadow of death: to direct our feet into the way of peace.

~

WEDNESDAY DECEMBER 25, 2024
VIGIL MASS

First Reading: Isaiah 62: 1-5

Responsorial Psalm: Psalms 89: 4-5, 16-17, 27, 29

Second Reading: Acts 13: 16-17, 22-25

Gospel: Matthew 1: 1-25

First Reading: Isaiah 62: 1-5

1 For Sion's sake I will not hold my peace, and for the sake of Jerusalem, I will not rest till her just one come forth as brightness, and her saviour be lighted as a lamp.

2 And the Gentiles shall see thy just one, and all kings thy glorious one: and thou shalt be called by a new name, which the mouth of the Lord shall name.

3 And thou shalt be a crown of glory in the hand of the Lord, and a royal diadem in the hand of thy God.

4 Thou shalt no more be called Forsaken: and thy land shall no more be called Desolate: but thou shalt be called My pleasure in her, and thy land inhabited. Because the Lord hath been well pleased with thee: and thy land shall be inhabited.

5 For the young man shall dwell with the virgin, and thy children shall dwell in thee. And the bridegroom shall rejoice over the bride, and thy God shall rejoice over thee.

Responsorial Psalm: Psalms 89: 4-5, 16-17, 27, 29

R. (2a) For ever I will sing the goodness of the Lord.

4 I have made a covenant with my elect: I have sworn to David my servant:

5 Thy seed will I settle for ever. And I will build up thy throne unto generation and generation.

R. For ever I will sing the goodness of the Lord.

16 Blessed is the people that knoweth jubilation. They shall walk, O Lord, in the light of thy countenance:

17 And in thy name they shall rejoice all the day, and in thy justice they shall be exalted.

R. For ever I will sing the goodness of the Lord.

27 He shall cry out to me: Thou art my father: my God, and the support of my salvation.

29 I will keep my mercy for him for ever: and my covenant faithful to him.

R. For ever I will sing the goodness of the Lord.

Second Reading: Acts 13: 16-17, 22-25

16 Then Paul rising up, and with his hand bespeaking silence, said: Ye men of Israel, and you that fear God, give ear.

17 The God of the people of Israel chose our fathers, and exalted the people when they were sojourners in the land of Egypt, and with an high arm brought them out from thence,

22 And when he had removed him, he raised them up David to be king: to whom giving testimony, he said: I have found David, the son of Jesse, a man according to my own heart, who shall do all my wills.

23 Of this man's seed God according to his promise, hath raised up to Israel a Saviour, Jesus:

24 John first preaching, before his coming, the baptism of penance to all the people of Israel.

25 And when John was fulfilling his course, he said: I am not he, whom you think me to be: but behold, there cometh one after me, whose shoes of his feet I am not worthy to loose.

Alleluia

R. Alleluia, alleluia.

Tomorrow the wickedness of the earth will be destroyed: the Savior of the world will reign over us.

R. Alleluia, alleluia.

Gospel: Matthew 1: 1-25

1 The book of the generation of Jesus Christ, the son of David, the son of Abraham:

2 Abraham begot Isaac. And Isaac begot Jacob. And Jacob begot Judas and his brethren.

3 And Judas begot Phares and Zara of Thamar. And Phares begot Esron. And Esron begot Aram.

4 And Aram begot Aminadab. And Aminadab begot Naasson. And Naasson begot Salmon.

5 And Salmon begot Booz of Rahab. And Booz begot Obed of Ruth. And Obed begot Jesse.

6 And Jesse begot David the king. And David the king begot Solomon, of her that had been the wife of Urias.

7 And Solomon begot Roboam. And Roboam begot Abia. And Abia begot Asa.

8 And Asa begot Josaphat. And Josaphat begot Joram. And Joram begot Ozias.

9 And Ozias begot Joatham. And Joatham begot Achaz. And Achaz begot Ezechias.

10 And Ezechias begot Manasses. And Manasses begot Amon. And Amon begot Josias.

11 And Josias begot Jechonias and his brethren in the transmigration of Babylon.

12 And after the transmigration of Babylon, Jechonias begot Salathiel. And Salathiel begot Zorobabel.

13 And Zorobabel begot Abiud. And Abiud begot Eliacim. And Eliacim begot Azor.

14 And Azor begot Sadoc. And Sadoc begot Achim. And Achim begot Eliud.

15 And Eliud begot Eleazar. And Eleazar begot Mathan. And Mathan begot Jacob.

16 And Jacob begot Joseph the husband of Mary, of whom was born Jesus, who is called Christ.

17 So all the generations, from Abraham to David, are fourteen generations. And from David to the transmigration of Babylon, are fourteen generations: and from the transmigration of Babylon to Christ are fourteen generations.

18 Now the generation of Christ was in this wise. When as his mother Mary was espoused to Joseph, before they came together, she was found with child, of the Holy Ghost.

19 Whereupon Joseph her husband, being a just man, and not willing publicly to expose her, was minded to put her away privately.

20 But while he thought on these things, behold the angel of the Lord appeared to him in his sleep, saying: Joseph, son of David, fear not to take unto thee Mary thy wife, for that which is conceived in her, is of the Holy Ghost.

21 And she shall bring forth a son: and thou shalt call his name JESUS. For he shall save his people from their sins.

22 Now all this was done that it might be fulfilled which the Lord spoke by the prophet, saying:

23 Behold a virgin shall be with child, and bring forth a son, and they shall call his name Emmanuel, which being interpreted is, God with us.

24 And Joseph rising up from sleep, did as the angel of the Lord had commanded him, and took unto him his wife.

25 And he knew her not till she brought forth her firstborn son: and he called his name JESUS.

~

WEDNESDAY DECEMBER 25, 2024
MIDNIGHT MASS

First Reading: Isaiah 9: 1-6

Responsorial Psalm: Psalms 96: 1-2, 2-3, 11-12, 13

Second Reading: Titus 2: 11-14

Alleluia: Luke 2: 10-11

Gospel: Luke 2: 1-14

First Reading: Isaiah 9: 1-6

1 The people that walked in darkness, have seen a great light: to them that dwelt in the region of the shadow of death, light is risen.

2 Thou hast multiplied the nation, and hast not increased the joy. They shall rejoice before thee, as they that rejoice in the harvest, as conquerors rejoice after taking a prey, when they divide the spoils.

3 For the yoke of their burden, and the rod of their shoulder, and the sceptre of their oppressor thou hast overcome, as in the day of Median.

4 For every violent taking of spoils, with tumult, and garment mingled with blood, shall be burnt, and be fuel for the fire.

5 For a CHILD IS BORN to us, and a son is given to us, and the government is upon his shoulder: and his name shall be called, Wonderful, Counsellor, God the Mighty, the Father of the world to come, the Prince of Peace.

6 His empire shall be multiplied, and there shall be no end of peace: he shall sit upon the throne of David, and upon his kingdom; to establish it and strengthen it with judgment and with justice, from henceforth and for ever: the zeal of the Lord of hosts will perform this.

Responsorial Psalm: Psalms 96: 1-2, 2-3, 11-12, 13

R. (Luke 2:11) Today is born our Savior, Christ the Lord.

1 Sing ye to the Lord a new canticle: sing to the Lord, all the earth.

2a Sing ye to the Lord and bless his name.

R. Today is born our Savior, Christ the Lord.

∽

First Reading: Isaiah 62: 11-12

Responsorial Psalm: Psalms 97: 1, 6, 11-12

Second Reading: Titus 3: 4-7

Alleluia: Luke 2: 14

Gospel: Luke 2: 15-20

First Reading: Isaiah 62: 11-12

11 Behold the Lord hath made it to be heard in the ends of the earth, tell the daughter of Sion: Behold thy Saviour cometh: behold his reward is with him, and his work before him.

12 And they shall call them, The holy people, the redeemed of the Lord. But thou shalt be called: A city sought after, and not forsaken.

Responsorial Psalm: Psalms 97: 1, 6, 11-12

R. A light will shine on us this day: the Lord is born for us.

1 The Lord hath reigned, let the earth rejoice: let many islands be glad.

6 The heavens declared his justice: and all people saw his glory.

R. A light will shine on us this day: the Lord is born for us.

11 Light is risen to the just, and joy to the right of heart.

12 Rejoice, ye just, in the Lord: and give praise to the remembrance of his holiness.

R. A light will shine on us this day: the Lord is born for us.

Second Reading: Titus 3: 4-7

4 But when the goodness and kindness of God our Saviour appeared:

5 Not by the works of justice, which we have done, but according to his mercy, he saved us, by the laver of regeneration, and renovation of the Holy

Ghost;

6 Whom he hath poured forth upon us abundantly, through Jesus Christ our Saviour:

7 That, being justified by his grace, we may be heirs, according to hope of life everlasting.

Alleluia: Luke 2: 14

R. Alleluia, alleluia.

14 Glory to God in the highest, and on earth peace to those on whom his favor rests.

R. Alleluia, alleluia.

Gospel: Luke 2: 15-20

15 And it came to pass, after the angels departed from them into heaven, the shepherds said one to another: Let us go over to Bethlehem, and let us see this word that is come to pass, which the Lord hath shewed to us.

16 And they came with haste; and they found Mary and Joseph, and the infant lying in the manger.

17 And seeing, they understood of the word that had been spoken to them concerning this child.

18 And all that heard, wondered; and at those things that were told them by the shepherds.

19 But Mary kept all these words, pondering them in her heart.

20 And the shepherds returned, glorifying and praising God, for all the things they had heard and seen, as it was told unto them.

~

WEDNESDAY DECEMBER 25, 2024
DAYTIME MASS

First Reading: Isaiah 52: 7-10

Responsorial Psalm: Psalms 98: 1, 2-3, 3-4, 5-6

Second Reading: Hebrews 1: 1-6

Gospel: John 1: 1-18

First Reading: Isaiah 52: 7-10

7 How beautiful upon the mountains are the feet of him that bringeth good tidings, and that preacheth peace: of him that sheweth forth good, that preacheth salvation, that saith to Sion: Thy God shall reign!

8 The voice of thy watchmen: they have lifted up their voice, they shall praise together: for they shall see eye to eye when the Lord shall convert Sion.

9 Rejoice, and give praise together, O ye deserts of Jerusalem: for the Lord hath comforted his people: he hath redeemed Jerusalem.

10 The Lord hath prepared his holy arm in the sight of all the Gentiles: and all the ends of the earth shall see the salvation of our God.

Responsorial Psalm: Psalms 98: 1, 2-3, 3-4, 5-6

R. (3c) All the ends of the earth have seen the saving power of God.

1 Sing ye to the Lord anew canticle: because he hath done wonderful things. His right hand hath wrought for him salvation, and his arm is holy.

R. All the ends of the earth have seen the saving power of God.

2 The Lord hath made known his salvation: he hath revealed his justice in the sight of the Gentiles.

3ab He hath remembered his mercy his truth toward the house of Israel.

R. All the ends of the earth have seen the saving power of God.

3cd All the ends of the earth have seen the salvation of our God.

4 Sing joyfully to God, all the earth; make melody, rejoice and sing.

R. All the ends of the earth have seen the saving power of God.

5 Sing praise to the Lord on the harp, on the harp, and with the voice of a psalm:

6 With long trumpets, and sound of comet. Make a joyful noise before the Lord our king:

R. All the ends of the earth have seen the saving power of God.

Second Reading: Hebrews 1: 1-6

1 God, who, at sundry times and in divers manners, spoke in times past to the fathers by the prophets, last of all,

2 In these days hath spoken to us by his Son, whom he hath appointed heir of all things, by whom also he made the world.

3 Who being the brightness of his glory, and the figure of his substance, and upholding all things by the word of his power, making purgation of sins, sitteth on the right hand of the majesty on high.

4 Being made so much better than the angels, as he hath inherited a more excellent name than they.

5 For to which of the angels hath he said at any time, Thou art my Son, today have I begotten thee? And again, I will be to him a Father, and he shall be to me a Son?

6 And again, when he bringeth in the first begotten into the world, he saith: And let all the angels of God adore him.

Alleluia

R. Alleluia, alleluia.

A holy day has dawned upon us. Come, you nations, and adore the Lord. For today a great light has come upon the earth.

R. Alleluia, alleluia.

Gospel: John 1: 1-18

1 In the beginning was the Word, and the Word was with God, and the Word was God.

2 The same was in the beginning with God.

3 All things were made by him: and without him was made nothing that was made.

4 In him was life, and the life was the light of men.

5 And the light shineth in darkness, and the darkness did not comprehend it.

6 There was a man sent from God, whose name was John.

7 This man came for a witness, to give testimony of the light, that all men might believe through him.

8 He was not the light, but was to give testimony of the light.

9 That was the true light, which enlighteneth every man that cometh into this world.

10 He was in the world, and the world was made by him, and the world knew him not.

11 He came unto his own, and his own received him not.

12 But as many as received him, he gave them power to be made the sons of God, to them that believe in his name.

13 Who are born, not of blood, nor of the will of the flesh, nor of the will of man, but of God.

14 And the Word was made flesh, and dwelt among us, (and we saw his glory, the glory as it were of the only begotten of the Father,) full of grace and truth.

15 John beareth witness of him, and crieth out, saying: This was he of whom I spoke: He that shall come after me, is preferred before me: because he was before me.

16 And of his fulness we all have received, and grace for grace.

17 For the law was given by Moses; grace and truth came by Jesus Christ.

18 No man hath seen God at any time: the only begotten Son who is in the bosom of the Father, he hath declared him.

~

THURSDAY DECEMBER 26, 2024

First Reading: Acts 6: 8-10; 7: 54-59

Responsorial Psalm: Psalms 31: 3cd-4, 6 and 8ab, 16bc and 17

Alleluia: Psalms 118: 26a, 27a

Gospel: Matthew 10: 17-22

First Reading: Acts 6: 8-10; 7: 54-59

8 And Stephen, full of grace and fortitude, did great wonders and signs among the people.

9 Now there arose some of that which is called the synagogue of the Libertines, and of the Cyrenians, and of the Alexandrians, and of them that were of Cilicia and Asia, disputing with Stephen.

10 And they were not able to resist the wisdom and the spirit that spoke.

7:54 Now hearing these things, they were cut to the heart, and they gnashed with their teeth at him.

55 But he, being full of the Holy Ghost, looking up steadfastly to heaven, saw the glory of God, and Jesus standing on the right hand of God.

56 And he said: Behold, I see the heavens opened, and the Son of man standing on the right hand of God.

57 And they crying out with a loud voice, stopped their ears, and with one accord ran violently upon him.

58 And casting him forth without the city, they stoned him; and the witnesses laid down their garments at the feet of a young man, whose name was Saul.

59 And they stoned Stephen, invoking, and saying: Lord Jesus, receive my spirit.

Responsorial Psalm: Psalms 31: 3cd-4, 6 and 8ab, 16bc and 17

R. (6) Into your hands, O Lord, I commend my spirit.

3cd Be thou unto me a God, a protector, and a house of refuge, to save me.

4 For thou art my strength and my refuge; and for thy name's sake thou wilt lead me, and nourish me.

R. Into your hands, O Lord, I commend my spirit.

6 Into thy hands I commend my spirit: thou hast redeemed me, O Lord, the God of truth.

8ab I will be glad and rejoice in thy mercy.

R. Into your hands, O Lord, I commend my spirit.

16bc Deliver me out of the hands of my enemies; and from them that persecute me.

17 Make thy face to shine upon thy servant; save me in thy mercy.

R. Into your hands, O Lord, I commend my spirit.

Alleluia: Psalms 118: 26a, 27a

R. Alleluia, alleluia.

26a, 27a Blessed is he who comes in the name of the LORD: the LORD is God and has given us light.

R. Alleluia, alleluia.

Gospel: Matthew 10: 17-22

17 But beware of men. For they will deliver you up in councils, and they will scourge you in their synagogues.

18 And you shall be brought before governors, and before kings for my sake, for a testimony to them and to the Gentiles:

19 But when they shall deliver you up, take no thought how or what to speak: for it shall be given you in that hour what to speak.

20 For it is not you that speak, but the Spirit of your Father that speaketh in you.

21 The brother also shall deliver up the brother to death, and the father the son: and the children shall rise up against their parents, and shall put them to death.

22 And you shall be hated by all men for my name's sake: but he that shall persevere unto the end, he shall be saved.

～

FRIDAY DECEMBER 27, 2024

First Reading: First John 1: 1-4

Responsorial Psalm: Psalms 97: 1-2, 5-6, 11-12

Gospel: John 20: 1a and 2-8

First Reading: First John 1: 1-4

1 That which was from the beginning, which we have heard, which we have seen with our eyes, which we have looked upon, and our hands have handled, of the word of life:

2 For the life was manifested; and we have seen and do bear witness, and declare unto you the life eternal, which was with the Father, and hath appeared to us:

3 That which we have seen and have heard, we declare unto you, that you also may have fellowship with us, and our fellowship may be with the Father, and with his Son Jesus Christ.

4 And these things we write to you, that you may rejoice, and your joy may be full.

Responsorial Psalm: Psalms 97: 1-2, 5-6, 11-12

R. (12) Rejoice in the Lord, you just!

1 The Lord hath reigned, let the earth rejoice: let many islands be glad.

2 Clouds and darkness are round about him: justice and judgment are the establishment of his throne.

R. Rejoice in the Lord, you just!

5 The mountains melted like wax, at the presence of the Lord: at the presence of the Lord of all the earth.

6 The heavens declared his justice: and all people saw his glory.

R. Rejoice in the Lord, you just!

11 Light is risen to the just, and joy to the right of heart.

12 Rejoice, ye just, in the Lord: and give praise to the remembrance of his holiness.

R. Rejoice in the Lord, you just!

Alleluia: See Te Deum

R. Alleluia, alleluia.

We praise you, O God, we acclaim you as Lord; the glorious company of Apostles praise you.

R. Alleluia, alleluia.

Gospel: John 20: 1a and 2-8

1a And on the first day of the week,

2 Mary Magdalen ran, therefore, and cometh to Simon Peter, and to the other disciple whom Jesus loved, and saith to them: They have taken away the Lord out of the sepulchre, and we know not where they have laid him.

3 Peter therefore went out, and that other disciple, and they came to the sepulchre.

4 And they both ran together, and that other disciple did outrun Peter, and came first to the sepulchre.

5 And when he stooped down, he saw the linen cloths lying; but yet he went not in.

6 Then cometh Simon Peter, following him, and went into the sepulchre, and saw the linen cloths lying,

7 And the napkin that had been about his head, not lying with the linen cloths, but apart, wrapped up into one place.

8 Then that other disciple also went in, who came first to the sepulchre: and he saw, and believed.

~

SATURDAY DECEMBER 28, 2024

First Reading: First John 1: 5 – 2: 2

Responsorial Psalm: Psalms 124: 2-3, 4-5, 7b-8

Gospel: Matthew 2: 13-18

First Reading: First John 1: 5 – 2: 2

5 And this is the declaration which we have heard from him, and declare unto you: That God is light, and in him there is no darkness.

6 If we say that we have fellowship with him, and walk in darkness, we lie, and do not the truth.

7 But if we walk in the light, as he also is in the light, we have fellowship one with another, and the blood of Jesus Christ his Son cleanseth us from all sin.

8 If we say that we have no sin, we deceive ourselves, and the truth is not in us.

9 If we confess our sins, he is faithful and just, to forgive us our sins, and to cleanse us from all iniquity.

10 If we say that we have not sinned, we make him a liar, and his word is not in us.

2:1 My little children, these things I write to you, that you may not sin. But if any man sin, we have an advocate with the Father, Jesus Christ the just:

2 And he is the propitiation for our sins: and not for ours only, but also for those of the whole world.

Responsorial Psalm: Psalms 124: 2-3, 4-5, 7b-8

R. (7) Our soul has been rescued like a bird from the fowler's snare.

2 If it had not been that the Lord was with us, When men rose up against us,

3 Perhaps they had swallowed us up alive. When their fury was enkindled against us,

R. Our soul has been rescued like a bird from the fowler's snare.

4 Perhaps the waters had swallowed us up.

5 Our soul hath passed through a torrent: perhaps our soul had passed through a water insupportable.

R. Our soul has been rescued like a bird from the fowler's snare.

7b The snare is broken, and we are delivered.

8 Our help is in the name of the Lord, who made heaven and earth.

R. Our soul has been rescued like a bird from the fowler's snare.

Alleluia: See Te Deum

R. Alleluia, alleluia.

We praise you, O God, we acclaim you as Lord; the white-robed army of martyrs praise you.

R. Alleluia, alleluia.

Gospel: Matthew 2: 13-18

13 And after they were departed, behold an angel of the Lord appeared in sleep to Joseph, saying: Arise, and take the child and his mother, and fly into Egypt: and be there until I shall tell thee. For it will come to pass that Herod will seek the child to destroy him.

14 Who arose, and took the child and his mother by night, and retired into Egypt: and he was there until the death of Herod:

15 That it might be fulfilled which the Lord spoke by the prophet, saying: Out of Egypt have I called my son.

16 Then Herod perceiving that he was deluded by the wise men, was exceeding angry; and sending killed all the men children that were in Bethlehem, and in all the borders thereof, from two years old and under, according to the time which he had diligently inquired of the wise men.

17 Then was fulfilled that which was spoken by Jeremias the prophet, saying:

18 A voice in Rama was heard, lamentation and great mourning; Rachel bewailing her children, and would not be comforted, because they are not.

~

SUNDAY DECEMBER 29, 2024

First Reading: First Samuel 1: 20-22, 24-28 or Sirach 3: 2-6, 12-14

Responsorial Psalm: Psalms 84: 2-3, 5-6, 9-10 or Psalms 128: 1-2, 3, 4-5

Second Reading: First John 3: 1-2, 21-24 or Colossians 3: 12-21

Alleluia: Colossians 3: 15a, 16a or Acts 16: 14b

Gospel: Luke 2: 41-52

First Reading: First Samuel 1: 20-22, 24-28 or Sirach 3: 2-6, 12-14

20 And it came to pass when the time was come about, Anna conceived and bore a son, and called his name Samuel: because she had asked him of the Lord.

21 And Elcana her husband went up, and all his house, to offer to the Lord the solemn sacrifice, and his vow.

22 But Anna went not up: for she said to her husband: I will not go till the child be weaned, and till I may carry him, that he may appear before the Lord, and may abide always there.

24 And after she had weaned him, she carried him with her, with three calves, and three bushels of flour, and a bottle of wine, and she brought him to the house of the Lord in Silo. Now the child was as yet very young:

25 And they immolated a calf, and offered the child to Heli.

26 And Anna said: I beseech thee, my lord, as thy soul liveth, my lord: I am that woman who stood before thee here praying to the Lord.

27 For this child did I pray, and the Lord hath granted me my petition, which I asked of him.

28 Therefore I also have lent him to the Lord all the days of his life, he shall be lent to the Lord. And they adored the Lord there. And Anna prayed, and said:

Or

2 For God hath made the father honourable to the children: and seeking the judgment of the mothers, hath confirmed it upon the children.

3 He that loveth God, shall obtain pardon for his sins by prayer, and shall refrain himself from them, and shall be heard in the prayer of days.

4 And he that honoureth his mother is as one that layeth up a treasure.

5 He that honoureth his father shall have joy in his own children, and in the day of his prayer he shall be heard.

6 He that honoureth his father shall enjoy a long life: and he that obeyeth the father, shall be a comfort to his mother.

12 Son, support the old age of thy father, and grieve him not in his life;

13 And if his understanding fail, have patience with him, and despise him not when thou art in thy strength: for the relieving of the father shall not be forgotten.

14 For good shall be repaid to thee for the sin of thy mother.

Responsorial Psalm: Psalms 84: 2-3, 5-6, 9-10 or Psalms 128: 1-2, 3, 4-5

R. (5a) Blessed are they who dwell in your house, O Lord.

2 How lovely are thy tabernacles, O Lord of host!

3 My soul longeth and fainteth for the courts of the Lord. My heart and my flesh have rejoiced in the living God.

R. Blessed are they who dwell in your house, O Lord.

5 Blessed are they that dwell in thy house, O Lord: they shall praise thee for ever and ever.

6 Blessed is the man whose help is from thee: in his heart he hath disposed to ascend by steps,

R. Blessed are they who dwell in your house, O Lord.

9 O Lord God of hosts, hear my prayer: give ear, O God of Jacob.

10 Behold, O God our protector: and look on the face of thy Christ.

R. Blessed are they who dwell in your house, O Lord.

Or

R. (1) Blessed are those who fear the Lord and walk in his ways.

1 Blessed are all they that fear the Lord: that walk in his ways.

2 For thou shalt eat the labours of thy hands: blessed art thou, and it shall be well with thee.

R. Blessed are those who fear the Lord and walk in his ways.

3 Thy wife as a fruitful vine, on the sides of thy house.

R. Blessed are those who fear the Lord and walk in his ways.

4 Behold, thus shall the man be blessed that feareth the Lord.

5 May the Lord bless thee out of Sion: and mayest thou see the good things of Jerusalem all the days of thy life.

R. Blessed are those who fear the Lord and walk in his ways.

Second Reading: First John 3: 1-2, 21-24 or Colossians 3: 12-21

1 Behold what manner of charity the Father hath bestowed upon us, that we should be called, and should be the sons of God. Therefore the world knoweth not us, because it knew not him.

2 Dearly beloved, we are now the sons of God; and it hath not yet appeared what we shall be. We know, that, when he shall appear, we shall be like to him: because we shall see him as he is.

21 Dearly beloved, if our heart do not reprehend us, we have confidence towards God:

22 And whatsoever we shall ask, we shall receive of him: because we keep his commandments, and do those things which are pleasing in his sight.

23 And this is his commandment, that we should believe in the name of his Son Jesus Christ: and love one another, as he hath given commandment unto us.

24 And he that keepeth his commandments, abideth in him, and he in him. And in this we know that he abideth in us, by the Spirit which he hath given us.

Or

12 Put ye on therefore, as the elect of God, holy, and beloved, the bowels of mercy, benignity, humility, modesty, patience:

13 Bearing with one another, and forgiving one another, if any have a complaint against another: even as the Lord hath forgiven you, so do you also.

14 But above all these things have charity, which is the bond of perfection:

15 And let the peace of Christ rejoice in your hearts, wherein also you are called in one body: and be ye thankful.

16 Let the word of Christ dwell in you abundantly, in all wisdom: teaching and admonishing one another in psalms, hymns, and spiritual canticles, singing in grace in your hearts to God.

17 All whatsoever you do in word or in work, do all in the name of the Lord Jesus Christ, giving thanks to God and the Father by him.

18 Wives, be subject to your husbands, as it behoveth in the Lord.

19 Husbands, love your wives, and be not bitter towards them.

20 Children, obey your parents in all things: for this is well pleasing to the Lord.

21 Fathers, provoke not your children to indignation, lest they be discouraged.

Alleluia: Colossians 3: 15a, 16a or Acts 16: 14b

R. Alleluia, alleluia.

15a, 16a Let the peace of Christ control your hearts; Let the word of Christ dwell in you richly.

R. Alleluia, alleluia.

Or

R. Alleluia, alleluia.

14b Open our hearts, O Lord, to listen to the words of your Son.

R. Alleluia, alleluia.

Gospel: Luke 2: 41-52

41 And his parents went every year to Jerusalem, at the solemn day of the pasch,

42 And when he was twelve years old, they going up into Jerusalem, according to the custom of the feast,

43 And having fulfilled the days, when they returned, the child Jesus remained in Jerusalem; and his parents knew it not.

44 And thinking that he was in the company, they came a day's journey, and sought him among their kinsfolks and acquaintance.

45 And not finding him, they returned into Jerusalem, seeking him.

46 And it came to pass, that, after three days, they found him in the temple, sitting in the midst of the doctors, hearing them, and asking them questions.

47 And all that heard him were astonished at his wisdom and his answers.

48 And seeing him, they wondered. And his mother said to him: Son, why hast thou done so to us? behold thy father and I have sought thee sorrowing.

49 And he said to them: How is it that you sought me? did you not know, that I must be about my father's business?

50 And they understood not the word that he spoke unto them.

51 And he went down with them, and came to Nazareth, and was subject to them. And his mother kept all these words in her heart.

52 And Jesus advanced in wisdom, and age, and grace with God and men.

MONDAY DECEMBER 30, 2024

First Reading: First John 2: 12-17

Responsorial Psalm: Psalms 96: 7-8a, 8b-9, 10

Gospel: Luke 2: 36-40

First Reading: First John 2: 12-17

12 I write unto you, little children, because your sins are forgiven you for his name's sake.

13 I write unto you, fathers, because you have known him, who is from the beginning. I write unto you, young men, because you have overcome the wicked one.

14 I write unto you, babes, because you have known the Father. I write unto you, young men, because you are strong, and the word of God abideth in you, and you have overcome the wicked one.

15 Love not the world, nor the things which are in the world. If any man love the world, the charity of the Father is not in him.

16 For all that is in the world, is the concupiscence of the flesh, and the concupiscence of the eyes, and the pride of life, which is not of the Father, but is of the world.

17 And the world passeth away, and the concupiscence thereof: but he that doth the will of God, abideth for ever.

Responsorial Psalm: Psalms 96: 7-8a, 8b-9, 10

R. (11a) Let the heavens be glad and the earth rejoice!

7 Bring ye to the Lord, O ye kindreds of the Gentiles, bring ye to the Lord glory and honour:

8a Bring to the Lord glory unto his name.

R. Let the heavens be glad and the earth rejoice!

8b Bring up sacrifices, and come into his courts:

9 Adore ye the Lord in his holy court. Let all the earth be moved at his presence.

R. Let the heavens be glad and the earth rejoice!

10 Say ye among the Gentiles, the Lord hath reigned. For he hath corrected the world, which shall not be moved: he will judge the people with justice.

R. Let the heavens be glad and the earth rejoice!

Alleluia

R. Alleluia, alleluia.

A holy day has dawned upon us. Come, you nations, and adore the Lord. Today a great light has come upon the earth.

R. Alleluia, alleluia.

Gospel: Luke 2: 36-40

36 And there was one Anna, a prophetess, the daughter of Phanuel, of the tribe of Aser; she was far advanced in years, and had lived with her husband seven years from her virginity.

37 And she was a widow until fourscore and four years; who departed not from the temple, by fastings and prayers serving night and day.

38 Now she, at the same hour, coming in, confessed to the Lord; and spoke of him to all that looked for the redemption of Israel.

39 And after they had performed all things according to the law of the Lord, they returned into Galilee, to their city Nazareth.

40 And the child grew, and waxed strong, full of wisdom; and the grace of God was in him.

≈

TUESDAY DECEMBER 31, 2024

First Reading: First John 2: 18-21

Responsorial Psalm: Psalms 96: 1-2, 11-12, 13

Alleluia: John 1: 14a, 12a

Gospel: John 1: 1-18

First Reading: First John 2: 18-21

18 Little children, it is the last hour; and as you have heard that Antichrist cometh, even now there are become many Antichrists: whereby we know that it is the last hour.

19 They went out from us, but they were not of us. For if they had been of us, they would no doubt have remained with us; but that they may be manifest, that they are not all of us.

20 But you have the unction from the Holy One, and know all things.

21 I have not written to you as to them that know not the truth, but as to them that know it: and that no lie is of the truth.

Responsorial Psalm: Psalms 96: 1-2, 11-12, 13

R. (11a) Let the heavens be glad and the earth rejoice!

1 Sing ye to the Lord a new canticle: sing to the Lord, all the earth.

2 Sing ye to the Lord and bless his name: shew forth his salvation from day to day.

R. Let the heavens be glad and the earth rejoice!

11 Let the heavens rejoice, and let the earth be glad, let the sea be moved, and the fulness thereof:

12 The fields and all things that are in them shall be joyful. Then shall all the trees of the woods rejoice

R. Let the heavens be glad and the earth rejoice!

13 Before the face of the Lord, because he cometh: because he cometh to judge the earth. He shall judge the world with justice, and the people with his truth.

R. Let the heavens be glad and the earth rejoice!

Alleluia: John 1: 14a, 12a

R. Alleluia, alleluia.

14a, 12a The Word of God became flesh and dwelt among us. To those who accepted him he gave power to become the children of God.

R. Alleluia, alleluia.

Gospel: John 1: 1-18

1 In the beginning was the Word, and the Word was with God, and the Word was God.

2 The same was in the beginning with God.

3 All things were made by him: and without him was made nothing that was made.

4 In him was life, and the life was the light of men.

5 And the light shineth in darkness, and the darkness did not comprehend it.

6 There was a man sent from God, whose name was John.

7 This man came for a witness, to give testimony of the light, that all men might believe through him.

8 He was not the light, but was to give testimony of the light.

9 That was the true light, which enlighteneth every man that cometh into this world.

10 He was in the world, and the world was made by him, and the world knew him not.

11 He came unto his own, and his own received him not.

12 But as many as received him, he gave them power to be made the sons of God, to them that believe in his name.

13 Who are born, not of blood, nor of the will of the flesh, nor of the will of man, but of God.

14 And the Word was made flesh, and dwelt among us, (and we saw his glory, the glory as it were of the only begotten of the Father,) full of grace and truth.

15 John beareth witness of him, and crieth out, saying: This was he of whom I spoke: He that shall come after me, is preferred before me: because he was before me.

16 And of his fulness we all have received, and grace for grace.

17 For the law was given by Moses; grace and truth came by Jesus Christ.

18 No man hath seen God at any time: the only begotten Son who is in the bosom of the Father, he hath declared him.

REFLECTIONS

REFLECTIONS

Presentation at the Temple (1342)
Ambrogio Lorenzetti

JANUARY 2025

WEDNESDAY JANUARY 1, 2025

First Reading: Numbers 6: 22-27

Responsorial Psalm: Psalms 67: 2-3, 5, 6, 8

Second Reading: Galatians 4: 4-7

Alleluia: Hebrews 1: 1-2

Gospel: Luke 2: 16-21

First Reading: Numbers 6: 22-27

22 And the Lord spoke to Moses, saying:

23 Say to Aaron and his sons: Thus shall you bless the children of Israel, and you shall say to them:

24 The Lord bless thee, and keep thee.

25 The Lord shew his face to thee, and have mercy on thee.

26 The Lord turn his countenance to thee, and give thee peace.

27 And they shall invoke my name upon the children of Israel, and I will bless them.

Responsorial Psalm: Psalms 67: 2-3, 5, 6, 8

R. (2a) May God bless us in his mercy.

2 May God have mercy on us, and bless us: may he cause the light of his countenance to shine upon us, and may he have mercy on us.

3 That we may know thy way upon earth: thy salvation in all nations.

R. May God bless us in his mercy.

5 Let the nations be glad and rejoice: for thou judgest the people with justice, and directest the nations upon earth.

R. May God bless us in his mercy.

6 Let the people, O God, confess to thee: let all the people give praise to thee:

8 May God bless us: and all the ends of the earth fear him.

R. May God bless us in his mercy.

Second Reading: Galatians 4: 4-7

4 But when the fulness of the time was come, God sent his Son, made of a woman, made under the law:

5 That he might redeem them who were under the law: that we might receive the adoption of sons.

6 And because you are sons, God hath sent the Spirit of his Son into your hearts, crying: Abba, Father.

7 Therefore now he is not a servant, but a son. And if a son, an heir also through God.

Alleluia: Hebrews 1: 1-2

R. Alleluia, alleluia.

1-2 In the past God spoke to our ancestors through the prophets; in these last days, he has spoken to us through the Son.

R. Alleluia, alleluia.

Gospel: Luke 2: 16-21

16 And they came with haste; and they found Mary and Joseph, and the infant lying in the manger.

17 And seeing, they understood of the word that had been spoken to them concerning this child.

18 And all that heard, wondered; and at those things that were told them by the shepherds.

19 But Mary kept all these words, pondering them in her heart.

20 And the shepherds returned, glorifying and praising God, for all the things they had heard and seen, as it was told unto them.

21 And after eight days were accomplished, that the child should be circumcised, his name was called JESUS, which was called by the angel, before he was conceived in the womb.

~

THURSDAY JANUARY 2, 2025

First Reading: First John 2: 22-28

Responsorial Psalm: Psalms 98: 1, 2-3ab, 3cd-4

Alleluia: Hebrews 1: 1-2

Gospel: John 1: 19-28

First Reading: First John 2: 22-28

22 Who is a liar, but he who denieth that Jesus is the Christ? This is Antichrist, who denieth the Father, and the Son.

23 Whosoever denieth the Son, the same hath not the Father. He that confesseth the Son, hath the Father also.

24 As for you, let that which you have heard from the beginning, abide in you. If that abide in you, which you have heard from the beginning, you also shall abide in the Son, and in the Father.

25 And this is the promise which he hath promised us, life everlasting.

26 These things have I written to you, concerning them that seduce you.

27 And as for you, let the unction, which you have received from him, abide in you. And you have no need that any man teach you; but as his unction teacheth you of all things, and is truth, and is no lie. And as it hath taught you, abide in him.

28 And now, little children, abide in him, that when he shall appear, we may have confidence, and not be confounded by him at his coming.

Responsorial Psalm: Psalms 98: 1, 2-3ab, 3cd-4

R. (3cd) All the ends of the earth have seen the saving power of God.

1 Sing ye to the Lord a new canticle: because he hath done wonderful things. His right hand hath wrought for him salvation, and his arm is holy.

R. All the ends of the earth have seen the saving power of God.

2 The Lord hath made known his salvation: he hath revealed his justice in the sight of the Gentiles.

3ab He hath remembered his mercy and his truth toward the house of Israel.

R. All the ends of the earth have seen the saving power of God.

3cd All the ends of the earth have seen the salvation of our God.

4 Sing joyfully to God, all the earth; make melody, rejoice and sing.

R. All the ends of the earth have seen the saving power of God.

Alleluia: Hebrews 1: 1-2

R. Alleluia, alleluia.

1-2 In times past, God spoke to our ancestors through the prophets; in these last days, he has spoken to us through his Son.

R. Alleluia, alleluia.

Gospel: John 1: 19-28

19 And this is the testimony of John, when the Jews sent from Jerusalem priests and Levites to him, to ask him: Who art thou?

20 And he confessed, and did not deny: and he confessed: I am not the Christ.

21 And they asked him: What then? Art thou Elias? And he said: I am not. Art thou the prophet? And he answered: No.

22 They said therefore unto him: Who art thou, that we may give an answer to them that sent us? What sayest thou of thyself?

23 He said: I am the voice of one crying out in the wilderness, Make straight the way of the Lord, as said the prophet Isaias.

24 And they that were sent were of the Pharisees.

25 And they asked him, and said to him: Why then dost thou baptize, if thou be not Christ, nor Elias, nor the prophet?

26 John answered them, saying: I baptize with water; but there hath stood one in the midst of you, whom you know not.

27 The same is he that shall come after me, who is preferred before me: the latchet of whose shoe I am not worthy to loose.

28 These things were done in Bethania, beyond the Jordan, where John was baptizing.

~

FRIDAY JANUARY 3, 2025

First Reading: First John 2: 29 – 3: 6

Responsorial Psalm: Psalms 98: 1, 3cd-4, 5-6

Alleluia: John 1: 14a, 12a

Gospel: John 1: 29-34

First Reading: First John 2: 29 – 3: 6

29 If you know that he is just, know ye that every one also who doth justice is born of him.

3:1 Behold what manner of charity the Father hath bestowed upon us, that we should be called, and should be the sons of God. Therefore the world knoweth not us because it knew not him.

2 Dearly beloved, we are now the sons of God; and it hath not yet appeared

what we shall be. We know that when he shall appear, we shall be like to him because we shall see him as he is.

3 And every one that hath this hope in him sanctifieth himself as he also is holy.

4 Whosoever committeth sin committeth also iniquity; and sin is iniquity.

5 And you know that he appeared to take away our sins, and in him there is no sin.

6 Whosoever abideth in him sinneth not; and whosoever sinneth hath not seen him nor known him.

Responsorial Psalm: Psalms 98: 1, 3cd-4, 5-6

R. (3cd) All the ends of the earth have seen the saving power of God.

1 Sing ye to the Lord a new canticle because he hath done wonderful things. His right hand hath wrought for him salvation and his arm is holy.

R. All the ends of the earth have seen the saving power of God.

3cd All the ends of the earth have seen the salvation of our God.

4 Sing joyfully to God, all the earth; make melody, rejoice and sing.

R. All the ends of the earth have seen the saving power of God.

5 Sing praise to the Lord on the harp, on the harp, and with the voice of a psalm.

6 With long trumpets and sound of comet. Make a joyful noise before the Lord our king.

R. All the ends of the earth have seen the saving power of God.

Alleluia: John 1: 14a, 12a

R. Alleluia, alleluia.

14a, 12a The Word of God became flesh and dwelt among us. To those who accepted him he gave power to become the children of God.

R. Alleluia, alleluia.

Gospel: John 1: 29-34

29 The next day, John saw Jesus coming to him, and he saith: Behold the Lamb of God, behold him who taketh away the sin of the world.

30 This is he of whom I said: After me there cometh a man who is preferred before me because he was before me.

31 And I knew him not but that he may be made manifest in Israel, therefore am I come baptizing with water.

32 And John gave testimony, saying: I saw the Spirit coming down as a dove from heaven, and he remained upon him.

33 And I knew him not but he who sent me to baptize with water said to me: He upon whom thou shalt see the Spirit descending and remaining upon him, he it is that baptizeth with the Holy Ghost.

34 And I saw and I gave testimony that this is the Son of God.

SATURDAY JANUARY 4, 2025

First Reading: First John 3: 7-10

Responsorial Psalm: Psalms 98: 1, 7-8, 9

Alleluia: Hebrews 1: 1-2

Gospel: John 1: 35-42

First Reading: First John 3: 7-10

7 Little children, let no man deceive you. He that doth justice is just, even as he is just.

8 He that committeth sin is of the devil: for the devil sinneth from the beginning. For this purpose, the Son of God appeared, that he might destroy the works of the devil.

9 Whosoever is born of God, committeth not sin: for his seed abideth in him, and he cannot sin, because he is born of God.

10 In this the children of God are manifest, and the children of the devil. Whosoever is not just, is not of God, nor he that loveth not his brother.

Responsorial Psalm: Psalms 98: 1, 7-8, 9

R. (3cd) All the ends of the earth have seen the saving power of God.

1 Sing ye to the Lord a new canticle: because he hath done wonderful things. His right hand hath wrought for him salvation, and his arm is holy.

R. All the ends of the earth have seen the saving power of God.

7 Let the sea be moved and the fulness thereof: the world and they that dwell therein.

8 The rivers shall clap their hands, the mountains shall rejoice together.

R. All the ends of the earth have seen the saving power of God.

9 At the presence of the Lord: because he cometh to judge the earth. He shall judge the world with justice, and the people with equity.

R. All the ends of the earth have seen the saving power of God.

Alleluia: Hebrews 1: 1-2

R. Alleluia, alleluia.

1-2 In the past God spoke to our ancestors through the prophets: in these last days, he has spoken to us through the Son.

R. Alleluia, alleluia.

Gospel: John 1: 35-42

35 The next day again John stood, and two of his disciples.

36 And beholding Jesus walking, he saith: Behold the Lamb of God.

37 And the two disciples heard him speak, and they followed Jesus.

38 And Jesus turning, and seeing them following him, saith to them: What seek ye? Who said to him, Rabbi, (which is to say, being interpreted, Master,) where dwellest thou?

39 He saith to them: Come and see. They came, and saw where he abode, and they stayed with him that day: now it was about the tenth hour.

40 And Andrew, the brother of Simon Peter, was one of the two who had heard of John, and followed him.

41 He findeth first his brother Simon, and saith to him: We have found the Messias, which is, being interpreted, the Christ.

42 And he brought him to Jesus. And Jesus looking upon him, said: Thou art Simon the son of Jona: thou shalt be called Cephas, which is interpreted Peter.

~

SUNDAY JANUARY 5, 2025

First Reading: Isaiah 60: 1-6

Responsorial Psalm: Psalms 72: 1-2, 7-8, 10-11, 12-13

Second Reading: Ephesians 3: 2-3a, 5-6

Alleluia: Matthew 2: 2

Gospel: Matthew 2: 1-12

First Reading: Isaiah 60: 1-6

1 Arise, be enlightened, O Jerusalem: for thy light is come, and the glory of the Lord is risen upon thee.

2 For behold darkness shall cover the earth, and a mist the people: but the Lord shall arise upon thee, and his glory shall be seen upon thee.

3 And the Gentiles shall walk in thy light, and kings in the brightness of thy rising.

4 Lift up thy eyes round about, and see: all these are gathered together, they are come to thee: thy sons shall come from afar, and thy daughters shall rise up at thy side.

5 Then shalt thou see, and abound, and thy heart shall wonder and be enlarged, when the multitude of the sea shall be converted to thee, the strength of the Gentiles shall come to thee.

6 The multitude of camels shall cover thee, the dromedaries of Madian and Epha: all they from Saba shall come, bringing gold and frankincense: and showing forth praise to the Lord.

Responsorial Psalm: Psalms 72: 1-2, 7-8, 10-11, 12-13

R. (11) Lord, every nation on earth will adore you.

1-2 Give to the king thy judgment, O God: and to the king's son thy justice: To judge thy people with justice, and thy poor with judgment.

R. Lord, every nation on earth will adore you.

7 In his days shall justice spring up, and abundance of peace, till the moon be taken away.

8 And he shall rule from sea to sea, and from the river unto the ends of the earth.

R. Lord, every nation on earth will adore you.

10 The kings of Tharsis and the islands shall offer presents: the kings of the Arabians and of Saba shall bring gifts:

11 And all kings of the earth shall adore him: all nations shall serve him.

R. Lord, every nation on earth will adore you.

12 For he shall deliver the poor from the mighty: and the needy that had no helper.

13 He shall spare the poor and needy: and he shall save the souls of the poor.

R. Lord, every nation on earth will adore you.

Second Reading: Ephesians 3: 2-3a, 5-6

2 If yet you have heard of the dispensation of the grace of God which is given me towards you:

3a How that, according to revelation, the mystery has been made known to me.

5 Which in other generations was not known to the sons of men, as it is now revealed to his holy apostles and prophets in the Spirit:

6 That the Gentiles should be fellow heirs, and of the same body, and co-partners of his promise in Christ Jesus, by the gospel.

Alleluia: Matthew 2: 2

R. Alleluia, alleluia.

2 We saw his star at its rising and have come to do him homage.

R. Alleluia, alleluia.

Gospel: Matthew 2: 1-12

1 When Jesus therefore was born in Bethlehem of Juda, in the days of king Herod, behold, there came wise men from the east to Jerusalem.

2 Saying, Where is he that is born king of the Jews? For we have seen his star in the east, and are come to adore him.

3 And king Herod hearing this, was troubled, and all Jerusalem with him.

4 And assembling together all the chief priests and the scribes of the people, he inquired of them where Christ should be born.

5 But they said to him: In Bethlehem of Juda. For so it is written by the prophet:

6 And thou Bethlehem the land of Juda art not the least among the princes of Juda: for out of thee shall come forth the captain that shall rule my people Israel.

7 Then Herod, privately calling the wise men, learned diligently of them the time of the star which appeared to them;

8 And sending them into Bethlehem, said: Go and diligently inquire after the child, and when you have found him, bring me word again, that I also may come to adore him.

9 Who having heard the king, went their way; and behold the star which they had seen in the east, went before them, until it came and stood over where the child was.

10 And seeing the star they rejoiced with exceeding great joy.

11 And entering into the house, they found the child with Mary his mother, and falling down they adored him; and opening their treasures, they offered him gifts: gold, frankincense, and myrrh.

12 And having received an answer in sleep that they should not return to Herod, they went back another way into their country.

∼

MONDAY JANUARY 6, 2025

First Reading: First John 3: 22 – 4: 6

Responsorial Psalm: Psalms 2: 7bc-8, 10-11

Alleluia: Matthew 4: 23

Gospel: Matthew 4: 12-17, 23-25

First Reading: First John 3: 22 – 4: 6

22 And whatsoever we shall ask, we shall receive of him: because we keep his commandments, and do those things which are pleasing in his sight.

23 And this is his commandment, that we should believe in the name of his Son Jesus Christ: and love one another, as he hath given commandment unto us.

24 And he that keepeth his commandments, abideth in him, and he in him. And in this we know that he abideth in us, by the Spirit which he hath given us.

4:1 Dearly beloved, believe not every spirit, but try the spirits if they be of God: because many false prophets are gone out into the world.

2 By this is the spirit of God known. Every spirit which confesseth that Jesus Christ is come in the flesh, is of God:

3 And every spirit that dissolveth Jesus, is not of God: and this is Antichrist, of whom you have heard that he cometh, and he is now already in the world.

4 You are of God, little children, and have overcome him. Because greater is he that is in you, than he that is in the world.

5 They are of the world: therefore of the world they speak, and the world heareth them.

6 We are of God. He that knoweth God, heareth us. He that is not of God, heareth us not. By this we know the spirit of truth, and the spirit of error.

Responsorial Psalm: Psalms 2: 7bc-8, 10-11

R. (8ab) I will give you all the nations for an inheritance.

7bc The Lord hath said to me: Thou art my son, this day have I begotten thee.

8 Ask of me, and I will give thee the Gentiles for thy inheritance, and the utmost parts of the earth for thy possession.

R. I will give you all the nations for an inheritance.

10 And now, O ye kings, understand: receive instruction, you that judge the earth.

11 Serve ye the Lord with fear: and rejoice unto him with trembling.

R. I will give you all the nations for an inheritance.

Alleluia: Matthew 4: 23

R. Alleluia, alleluia.

23 Jesus proclaimed the Gospel of the Kingdom and cured every disease among the people.

R. Alleluia, alleluia.

Gospel: Matthew 4: 12-17, 23-25

12 And when Jesus had heard that John was delivered up, he retired into Galilee:

13 And leaving the city Nazareth, he came and dwelt in Capharnaum on the sea coast, in the borders of Zabulon and Nephthalim;

14 That it might be fulfilled which was said by Isaias the prophet:

15 Land of Zabulon and land of Nephthalim, the way of the sea beyond the Jordan, Galilee of the Gentiles:

16 The people that sat in darkness, hath seen great light: and to them that sat in the region of the shadow of death, light is sprung up.

17 From that time Jesus began to preach, and to say: Do penance, for the kingdom of heaven is at hand.

23 And Jesus went about all Galilee, teaching in their synagogues, and preaching the gospel of the kingdom: and healing all manner of sickness and every infirmity, among the people.

24 And his fame went throughout all Syria, and they presented to him all sick people that were taken with divers diseases and torments, and such as were possessed by devils, and lunatics, and those that had palsy, and he cured them:

25 And much people followed him from Galilee, and from Decapolis, and from Jerusalem, and from Judea, and from beyond the Jordan.

First Reading: First John 4: 7-10

Responsorial Psalm: Psalms 72: 1-2, 3-4, 7-8

Alleluia: Luke 4: 18

Gospel: Mark 6: 34-44

First Reading: First John 4: 7-10

7 Dearly beloved, let us love one another, for charity is of God. And every one that loveth, is born of God, and knoweth God.

8 He that loveth not, knoweth not God: for God is charity.

9 By this hath the charity of God appeared towards us, because God hath sent his only begotten Son into the world, that we may live by him.

10 In this is charity: not as though we had loved God, but because he hath first loved us, and sent his Son to be a propitiation for our sins.

Responsorial Psalm: Psalms 72: 1-2, 3-4, 7-8

R. (11) Lord, every nation on earth will adore you.

1-2 Give to the king thy judgment, O God: and to the king's son thy justice: To judge thy people with justice, and thy poor with judgment.

R. Lord, every nation on earth will adore you.

3 Let the mountains receive peace for the people: and the hills justice.

4 He shall judge the poor of the people, and he shall save the children of the poor: and he shall humble the oppressor.

R. Lord, every nation on earth will adore you.

7 In his days shall justice spring up, and abundance of peace, till the moon be taken away.

8 And he shall rule from sea to sea, and from the river unto the ends of the earth.

R. Lord, every nation on earth will adore you.

Alleluia: Luke 4: 18

R. Alleluia, alleluia.

18 The Lord has sent me to bring glad tidings to the poor and to proclaim liberty to captives.

R. Alleluia, alleluia.

Gospel: Mark 6: 34-44

34 And Jesus going out saw a great multitude: and he had compassion on them, because they were as sheep not having a shepherd, and he began to teach them many things.

35 And when the day was now far spent, his disciples came to him, saying: This is a desert place, and the hour is now past:

36 Send them away, that going into the next villages and towns, they may buy themselves meat to eat.

37 And he answering said to them: Give you them to eat. And they said to him: Let us go and buy bread for two hundred pence, and we will give them to eat.

38 And he saith to them: How many loaves have you? go and see. And when they knew, they say: Five, and two fishes.

39 And he commanded them that they should make them all sit down by companies upon the green grass.

40 And they sat down in ranks, by hundreds and by fifties.

41 And when he had taken the five loaves, and the two fishes: looking up to heaven, he blessed, and broke the loaves, and gave to his disciples to set before them: and the two fishes he divided among them all.

42 And they all did eat, and had their fill.

43 And they took up the leavings, twelve full baskets of fragments, and of the fishes.

44 And they that did eat, were five thousand men.

～

WEDNESDAY JANUARY 8, 2025

First Reading: First John 4: 11-18

Responsorial Psalm: Psalms 72: 1-2, 10, 12-13

Alleluia: First Timothy 3: 16

Gospel: Mark 6: 45-52

First Reading: First John 4: 11-18

11 My dearest, if God hath so loved us; we also ought to love one another.

12 No man hath seen God at any time. If we love one another, God abideth in us, and his charity is perfected in us.

13 In this we know that we abide in him, and he in us: because he hath given us of his spirit.

14 And we have seen, and do testify, that the Father hath sent his Son to be the Saviour of the world.

15 Whosoever shall confess that Jesus is the Son of God, God abideth in him, and he in God.

16 And we have known, and have believed the charity, which God hath to us. God is charity: and he that abideth in charity, abideth in God, and God in him.

17 In this is the charity of God perfected with us, that we may have confidence in the day of judgment: because as he is, we also are in this world.

18 Fear is not in charity: but perfect charity casteth out fear, because fear hath pain. And he that feareth, is not perfected in charity.

Responsorial Psalm: Psalms 72: 1-2, 10, 12-13

R. (11) Lord, every nation on earth will adore you.

1-2 Give to the king thy judgment, O God: and to the king's son thy justice: To judge thy people with justice, and thy poor with judgment.

R. Lord, every nation on earth will adore you.

10 The kings of Tharsis and the islands shall offer presents: the kings of the Arabians and of Saba shall bring gifts:

R. Lord, every nation on earth will adore you.

12 For he shall deliver the poor from the mighty: and the needy that had no helper.

13 He shall spare the poor and needy: and he shall save the souls of the poor.

R. Lord, every nation on earth will adore you.

Alleluia: First Timothy 3: 16

R. Alleluia, alleluia.

16 Glory to you, O Christ, proclaimed to the Gentiles. Glory to you, O Christ, believed in throughout the world.

R. Alleluia, alleluia.

Gospel: Mark 6: 45-52

45 And immediately he obliged his disciples to go up into the ship, that they might go before him over the water to Bethsaida, whilst he dismissed the people.

46 And when he had dismissed them, he went up to the mountain to pray.

47 And when it was late, the ship was in the midst of the sea, and himself alone on the land.

48 And seeing them labouring in rowing, (for the wind was against them,) and about the fourth watch of the night, he cometh to them walking upon the sea, and he would have passed by them.

49 But they seeing him walking upon the sea, thought it was an apparition, and they cried out.

50 For they all saw him, and were troubled. And immediately he spoke with them, and said to them: Have a good heart, it is I, fear ye not.

51 And he went up to them into the ship, and the wind ceased: and they were far more astonished within themselves:

52 For they understood not concerning the loaves; for their heart was blinded.

THURSDAY JANUARY 9, 2025

First Reading: First John 4: 19 – 5: 4

Responsorial Psalm: Psalms 72: 1-2, 14 and 15bc, 17

Alleluia: Luke 4: 18

Gospel: Luke 4: 14-22

First Reading: First John 4: 19 – 5: 4

19 Let us therefore love God, because God first hath loved us.

20 If any man say, I love God, and hateth his brother; he is a liar. For he that loveth not his brother, whom he seeth, how can he love God, whom he seeth not?

21 And this commandment we have from God, that he, who loveth God, love also his brother.

5:1 Whosoever believeth that Jesus is the Christ, is born of God. And every one that loveth him who begot, loveth him also who is born of him.

2 In this we know that we love the children of God: when we love God, and keep his commandments.

3 For this is the charity of God, that we keep his commandments: and his commandments are not heavy.

4 For whatsoever is born of God, overcometh the world: and this is the victory which overcometh the world, our faith.

Responsorial Psalm: Psalms 72: 1-2, 14 and 15bc, 17

R. (11) Lord, every nation on earth will adore you.

1-2 Give to the king thy judgment, O God: and to the king's son thy justice: To judge thy people with justice, and thy poor with judgment.

R. Lord, every nation on earth will adore you.

14 He shall redeem their souls from usuries and iniquity: and their names shall be honourable in his sight.

15bc For him they shall always adore: they shall bless him all the day.

R. Lord, every nation on earth will adore you.

17 Let his name be blessed for evermore: his name continueth before the sun. And in him shall all the tribes of the earth be blessed: all nations shall magnify him.

R. Lord, every nation on earth will adore you.

Alleluia: Luke 4: 18

R. Alleluia, alleluia.

18 The Lord has sent me to bring glad tidings to the poor and to proclaim liberty to captives.

R. Alleluia, alleluia.

Gospel: Luke 4: 14-22

14 And Jesus returned in the power of the spirit, into Galilee, and the fame of him went out through the whole country.

15 And he taught in their synagogues, and was magnified by all.

16 And he came to Nazareth, where he was brought up: and he went into the synagogue, according to his custom, on the sabbath day; and he rose up to read.

17 And the book of Isaias the prophet was delivered unto him. And as he unfolded the book, he found the place where it was written:

18 The Spirit of the Lord is upon me. Wherefore he hath anointed me to preach the gospel to the poor, he hath sent me to heal the contrite of heart,

19 To preach deliverance to the captives, and sight to the blind, to set at liberty them that are bruised, to preach the acceptable year of the Lord, and the day of reward.

20 And when he had folded the book, he restored it to the minister, and sat down. And the eyes of all in the synagogue were fixed on him.

21 And he began to say to them: This day is fulfilled this scripture in your ears.

22 And all gave testimony to him: and they wondered at the words of grace that proceeded from his mouth, and they said: Is not this the son of Joseph?

≈

First Reading: First John 5: 5-13

Responsorial Psalm: Psalms 147: 12-13, 14-15, 19-20

Alleluia: Matthew 4: 23

Gospel: Luke 5: 12-16

First Reading: First John 5: 5-13

5 Who is he that overcometh the world, but he that believeth that Jesus is the Son of God?

6 This is he that came by water and blood, Jesus Christ: not by water only, but by water and blood. And it is the Spirit which testifieth, that Christ is the truth.

7 And there are three who give testimony in heaven, the Father, the Word, and the Holy Ghost. And these three are one.

8 And there are three that give testimony on earth: the spirit, and the water, and the blood: and these three are one.

9 If we receive the testimony of men, the testimony of God is greater. For this is the testimony of God, which is greater, because he hath testified of his Son.

10 He that believeth in the Son of God, hath the testimony of God in himself. He that believeth not the Son, maketh him a liar: because he believeth not in the testimony which God hath testified of his Son.

11 And this is the testimony, that God hath given to us eternal life. And this life is in his Son.

12 He that hath the Son, hath life. He that hath not the Son, hath not life.

13 These things I write to you, that you may know that you have eternal life, you who believe in the name of the Son of God.

Responsorial Psalm: Psalms 147: 12-13, 14-15, 19-20

R. (12a) Praise the Lord, Jerusalem.

or

R. Alleluia.

12 Praise the Lord, O Jerusalem: praise thy God, O Sion.

13 Because he hath strengthened the bolts of thy gates, he hath blessed thy children within thee.

R. Praise the Lord, Jerusalem.

or

R. Alleluia.

14 Who hath placed peace in thy borders: and filleth thee with the fat of corn.

15 Who sendeth forth his speech to the earth: his word runneth swiftly.

R. Praise the Lord, Jerusalem.

or

R. Alleluia.

19 Who declareth his word to Jacob: his justices and his judgments to Israel.

20 He hath not done in like manner to every nation: and his judgments he hath not made manifest to them. Alleluia.

R. Praise the Lord, Jerusalem.

or

R. Alleluia.

Alleluia: Matthew 4: 23

R. Alleluia, alleluia.

23 Jesus proclaimed the Gospel of the Kingdom and cured every disease among the people.

R. Alleluia, alleluia.

Gospel: Luke 5: 12-16

12 And it came to pass, when he was in a certain city, behold a man full of leprosy, who seeing Jesus, and falling on his face, besought him, saying: Lord, if thou wilt, thou canst make me clean.

13 And stretching forth his hand, he touched him, saying: I will. Be thou cleansed. And immediately the leprosy departed from him.

14 And he charged him that he should tell no man, but, Go, shew thyself to the priest, and offer for thy cleansing according as Moses commanded, for a testimony to them.

15 But the fame of him went abroad the more, and great multitudes came together to hear, and to be healed by him of their infirmities.

16 And he retired into the desert, and prayed.

~

SATURDAY JANUARY 11, 2025

First Reading: First John 5: 14-21

Responsorial Psalm: Psalms 149: 1-2, 3-4, 5 and 6a and 9b

Alleluia: Matthew 4: 16

Gospel: John 3: 22-30

First Reading: First John 5: 14-21

14 And this is the confidence which we have towards him: That, whatsoever we shall ask according to his will, he heareth us.

15 And we know that he heareth us whatsoever we ask: we know that we have the petitions which we request of him.

16 He that knoweth his brother to sin a sin which is not to death, let him ask, and life shall be given to him, who sinneth not to death. There is a sin unto death: for that I say not that any man ask.

17 All iniquity is sin. And there is a sin unto death.

18 We know that whosoever is born of God, sinneth not: but the generation of God preserveth him, and the wicked one toucheth him not.

19 We know that we are of God, and the whole world is seated in wickedness.

20 And we know that the Son of God is come: and he hath given us understanding that we may know the true God, and may be in his true Son. This is the true God and life eternal.

21 Little children, keep yourselves from idols. Amen.

Responsorial Psalm: Psalms 149: 1-2, 3-4, 5 and 6a and 9b

R. (4a) The Lord takes delight in his people.

or

R. Alleluia.

1 Sing ye to the Lord a new canticle: let his praise be in the church of the saints.

2 Let Israel rejoice in him that made him: and let the children of Sion be joyful in their king.

R. The Lord takes delight in his people.

or

R. Alleluia.

3 Let them praise his name in choir: let them sing to him with the timbrel and the psaltery.

4 For the Lord is well pleased with his people: and he will exalt the meek unto salvation.

R. The Lord takes delight in his people.

or

R. Alleluia.

5 The saints shall rejoice in glory: they shall be joyful in their beds.

6a The high praise of God shall be in their mouth.

9b This glory is to all his saints. Alleluia.

R. The Lord takes delight in his people.

or

R. Alleluia.

Alleluia: Matthew 4: 16

R. Alleluia, alleluia.

16 The people who sit in darkness have seen a great light, on those dwelling in a land overshadowed by death light has arisen.

R. Alleluia, alleluia.

Gospel: John 3: 22-30

22 After these things Jesus and his disciples came into the land of Judea: and there he abode with them, and baptized.

23 And John also was baptizing in Ennon near Salim; because there was much water there; and they came and were baptized.

24 For John was not yet cast into prison.

25 And there arose a question between some of John's disciples and the Jews concerning purification:

26 And they came to John, and said to him: Rabbi, he that was with thee beyond the Jordan, to whom thou gavest testimony, behold he baptizeth, and all men come to him.

27 John answered, and said: A man cannot receive any thing, unless it be given him from heaven.

28 You yourselves do bear me witness, that I said, I am not Christ, but that I am sent before him.

29 He that hath the bride, is the bridegroom: but the friend of the bridegroom, who standeth and heareth him, rejoiceth with joy because of the bridegroom's voice. This my joy therefore is fulfilled.

30 He must increase, but I must decrease.

~

SUNDAY JANUARY 12, 2025

First Reading: Isaiah 42: 1-4, 6-7 or Isaiah 40: 1-5, 9-11

Responsorial Psalm: Psalms 104: 1b-2, 3-4, 24-25, 27-28, 29-30

Second Reading: Titus 2: 11-14; 3: 4-7

Alleluia: Luke 3: 16

Gospel: Luke 3: 15-16, 21-22

First Reading: Isaiah 42: 1-4, 6-7

1 Behold my servant, I will uphold him: my elect, my soul delighteth in him: I have given my spirit upon him, he shall bring forth judgment to the Gentiles.

2 He shall not cry, nor have respect to person, neither shall his voice be heard abroad.

3 The bruised reed he shall not break, and smoking flax he shall not quench: he shall bring forth judgment unto truth.

4 He shall not be sad, nor troublesome, till he set judgment in the earth: and the islands shall wait for his law.

6 I the Lord have called thee in justice, and taken thee by the hand, and preserved thee. And I have given thee for a covenant of the people, for a light of the Gentiles:

7 That thou mightest open the eyes of the blind, and bring forth the prisoner out of prison, and them that sit in darkness out of the prison house. Or

1 Be comforted, be comforted, my people, saith your God.

2 Speak ye to the heart of Jerusalem, and call to her: for her evil is come to an end, her iniquity is forgiven: she hath received of the hand of the Lord double for all her sins.

3 The voice of one crying in the desert: Prepare ye the way of the Lord, make straight in the wilderness the paths of our God.

4 Every valley shall be exalted, and every mountain and hill shall be made low, and the crooked shall become straight, and the rough ways plain.

5 And the glory of the Lord shall be revealed, and all flesh together shall see, that the mouth of the Lord hath spoken.

9 Get thee up upon a high mountain, thou that bringest good tidings to Sion: lift up thy voice with strength, thou that bringest good tidings to Jerusalem: lift it up, fear not. Say to the cities of Juda: Behold your God:

10 Behold the Lord God shall come with strength, and his arm shall rule: Behold his reward is with him and his work is before him.

11 He shall feed his flock like a shepherd: he shall gather together the lambs with his arm, and shall take them up in his bosom, and he himself shall carry them that are with young.

Responsorial Psalm: Psalms 104: 1b-2, 3-4, 24-25, 27-28, 29-30

R. (1) O bless the Lord, my soul.

1b O Lord my God, thou art exceedingly great. Thou hast put on praise and beauty:

2 And art clothed with light as with a garment. Who stretchest out the heaven like a pavilion:

R. O bless the Lord, my soul.

3 Who coverest the higher rooms thereof with water. Who makest the clouds thy chariot: who walkest upon the wings of the winds.

4 Who makest thy angels spirits: and thy ministers a burning fire.

R. O bless the Lord, my soul.

24 How great are thy works, O Lord? thou hast made all things in wisdom: the earth is filled with thy riches.

25 So is this great sea, which stretcheth wide its arms: there are creeping things without number: Creatures little and great.

R. O bless the Lord, my soul.

27 All expect of thee that thou give them food in season.

28 What thou givest to them they shall gather up: when thou openest thy hand, they shall all be filled with good.

R. O bless the Lord, my soul.

29 But if thou turnest away thy face, they shall be troubled: thou shalt take away their breath, and they shall fail, and shall return to their dust.

30 Thou shalt send forth thy spirit, and they shall be created: and thou shalt renew the face of the earth.

R. O bless the Lord, my soul.

Second Reading: Titus 2: 11-14; 3: 4-7

11 For the grace of God our Saviour hath appeared to all men;

12 Instructing us, that, denying ungodliness and worldly desires, we should live soberly, and justly, and godly in this world,

13 Looking for the blessed hope and coming of the glory of the great God and our Saviour Jesus Christ,

14 Who gave himself for us, that he might redeem us from all iniquity, and might cleanse to himself a people acceptable, a pursuer of good works.

3:4 But when the goodness and kindness of God our Saviour appeared:

5 Not by the works of justice, which we have done, but according to his mercy, he saved us, by the laver of regeneration, and renovation of the Holy Ghost;

6 Whom he hath poured forth upon us abundantly, through Jesus Christ our Saviour:

7 That, being justified by his grace, we may be heirs, according to hope of life everlasting.

Alleluia: Luke 3: 16

R. Alleluia, alleluia.

16 John said: One mightier than I is coming; he will baptize you with the Holy Spirit and with fire.

R. Alleluia, alleluia.

Gospel: Luke 3: 15-16, 21-22

15 And as the people were of opinion, and all were thinking in their hearts of John, that perhaps he might be the Christ;

16 John answered, saying unto all: I indeed baptize you with water; but there shall come one mightier than I, the latchet of whose shoes I am not worthy to loose: he shall baptize you with the Holy Ghost, and with fire:

21 Now it came to pass, when all the people were baptized, that Jesus also being baptized and praying, heaven was opened;

22 And the Holy Ghost descended in a bodily shape, as a dove upon him; and a voice came from heaven: Thou art my beloved Son; in thee I am well pleased.

~

First Reading: Hebrews 1: 1-6

Responsorial Psalm: Psalms 97: 1 and 2b, 6 and 7c, 9

Alleluia: Mark 1: 15

Gospel: Mark 1: 14-20

First Reading: Hebrews 1: 1-6

1 God, who, at sundry times and in divers manners, spoke in times past to the fathers by the prophets, last of all,

2 In these days hath spoken to us by his Son, whom he hath appointed heir of all things, by whom also he made the world.

3 Who being the brightness of his glory, and the figure of his substance, and upholding all things by the word of his power, making purgation of sins, sitteth on the right hand of the majesty on high.

4 Being made so much better than the angels, as he hath inherited a more excellent name than they.

5 For to which of the angels hath he said at any time, Thou art my Son, today have I begotten thee? And again, I will be to him a Father, and he shall be to me a Son?

6 And again, when he bringeth in the first begotten into the world, he saith: And let all the angels of God adore him.

Responsorial Psalm: Psalms 97: 1 and 2b, 6 and 7c, 9

R. (7c) Let all his angels worship him.

1 The Lord hath reigned, let the earth rejoice: let many islands be glad.

2b Justice and judgment are the establishment of his throne.

R. Let all his angels worship him.

6 The heavens declared his justice: and all people saw his glory.

7c Adore him, all you his angels:

R. Let all his angels worship him.

9 For thou art the most high Lord over all the earth: thou art exalted exceedingly above all gods.

R. Let all his angels worship him.

Alleluia: Mark 1: 15

R. Alleluia, alleluia.

15 The Kingdom of God is at hand; repent and believe in the Gospel.

R. Alleluia, alleluia.

Gospel: Mark 1: 14-20

14 And after that John was delivered up, Jesus came into Galilee, preaching the gospel of the kingdom of God,

15 And saying: The time is accomplished, and the kingdom of God is at hand: repent, and believe the gospel.

16 And passing by the sea of Galilee, he saw Simon and Andrew his brother, casting nets into the sea (for they were fishermen).

17 And Jesus said to them: Come after me, and I will make you to become fishers of men.

18 And immediately leaving their nets, they followed him.

19 And going on from thence a little farther, he saw James the son of Zebedee, and John his brother, who also were mending their nets in the ship:

20 And forthwith he called them. And leaving their father Zebedee in the ship with his hired men, they followed him.

~

TUESDAY JANUARY 14, 2025

First Reading: Hebrews 2: 5-12

Responsorial Psalm: Psalms 8: 2ab and 5, 6-7, 8-9

Alleluia: First Thessalonians 2: 13

Gospel: Mark 1: 21-28

First Reading: Hebrews 2: 5-12

5 For God hath not subjected unto angels the world to come, whereof we speak.

6 But one in a certain place hath testified, saying: What is man, that thou art mindful of him: or the son of man, that thou visitest him?

7 Thou hast made him a little lower than the angels: thou hast crowned him with glory and honour, and hast set him over the works of thy hands:

8 Thou hast subjected all things under his feet. For in that he hath subjected all things to him, he left nothing not subject to him. But now we see not as yet all things subject to him.

9 But we see Jesus, who was made a little lower than the angels, for the suffering of death, crowned with glory and honour: that, through the grace of God, he might taste death for all.

10 For it became him, for whom are all things, and by whom are all things, who had brought many children into glory, to perfect the author of their salvation, by his passion.

11 For both he that sanctifieth, and they who are sanctified, are all of one. For which cause he is not ashamed to call them brethren, saying:

12 I will declare thy name to my brethren; in the midst of the church will I praise thee.

Responsorial Psalm: Psalms 8: 2ab and 5, 6-7, 8-9

R. (7) You have given your Son rule over the works of your hands.

2ab O Lord our Lord, how admirable is thy name in the whole earth!

5 What is man that thou art mindful of him? or the son of man that thou visitest him?

R. You have given your Son rule over the works of your hands.

6 Thou hast made him a little less than the angels, thou hast crowned him with glory and honour:

7 And hast set him over the works of thy hands.

R. You have given your Son rule over the works of your hands.

8 Thou hast subjected all things under his feet, all sheep and oxen: moreover the beasts also of the fields.

9 The birds of the air, and the fishes of the sea, that pass through the paths of the sea.

R. You have given your Son rule over the works of your hands.

Alleluia: First Thessalonians 2: 13

R. Alleluia, alleluia.

13 Receive the word of God, not as the word of men, but as it truly is, the word of God.

R. Alleluia, alleluia.

Gospel: Mark 1: 21-28

21 And they entered into Capharnaum, and forthwith upon the sabbath days going into the synagogue, he taught them.

22 And they were astonished at his doctrine. For he was teaching them as one having power, and not as the scribes.

23 And there was in their synagogue a man with an unclean spirit; and he cried out,

24 Saying: What have we to do with thee, Jesus of Nazareth? art thou come to destroy us? I know who thou art, the Holy One of God.

25 And Jesus threatened him, saying: Speak no more, and go out of the man.

26 And the unclean spirit tearing him, and crying out with a loud voice, went out of him.

27 And they were all amazed, insomuch that they questioned among them-selves, saying: What thing is this? what is this new doctrine? for with power he commandeth even the unclean spirits, and they obey him.

28 And the fame of him was spread forthwith into all the country of Galilee.

WEDNESDAY JANUARY 15, 2025

First Reading: Hebrews 2: 14-18

Responsorial Psalm: Psalms 105: 1-2, 3-4, 6-7, 8-9

Alleluia: John 10: 27

Gospel: Mark 1: 29-39

First Reading: Hebrews 2: 5-12

5 For God hath not subjected unto angels the world to come, whereof we speak.

6 But one in a certain place hath testified, saying: What is man, that thou art mindful of him: or the son of man, that thou visitest him?

7 Thou hast made him a little lower than the angels: thou hast crowned him with glory and honour, and hast set him over the works of thy hands:

8 Thou hast subjected all things under his feet. For in that he hath subjected all things to him, he left nothing not subject to him. But now we see not as yet all things subject to him.

9 But we see Jesus, who was made a little lower than the angels, for the suffering of death, crowned with glory and honour: that, through the grace of God, he might taste death for all.

10 For it became him, for whom are all things, and by whom are all things, who had brought many children into glory, to perfect the author of their salvation, by his passion.

11 For both he that sanctifieth, and they who are sanctified, are all of one. For which cause he is not ashamed to call them brethren, saying:

12 I will declare thy name to my brethren; in the midst of the church will I praise thee.

Responsorial Psalm: Psalms 8: 2ab and 5, 6-7, 8-9

R. (7) You have given your Son rule over the works of your hands.

2ab O Lord our Lord, how admirable is thy name in the whole earth!

5 What is man that thou art mindful of him? or the son of man that thou visitest him?

R. You have given your Son rule over the works of your hands.

6 Thou hast made him a little less than the angels, thou hast crowned him with glory and honour:

7 And hast set him over the works of thy hands.

R. You have given your Son rule over the works of your hands.

8 Thou hast subjected all things under his feet, all sheep and oxen: moreover the beasts also of the fields.

9 The birds of the air, and the fishes of the sea, that pass through the paths of the sea.

R. You have given your Son rule over the works of your hands.

Alleluia: First Thessalonians 2: 13

R. Alleluia, alleluia.

13 Receive the word of God, not as the word of men, but as it truly is, the word of God.

R. Alleluia, alleluia.

Gospel: Mark 1: 21-28

21 And they entered into Capharnaum, and forthwith upon the sabbath days going into the synagogue, he taught them.

22 And they were astonished at his doctrine. For he was teaching them as one having power, and not as the scribes.

23 And there was in their synagogue a man with an unclean spirit; and he cried out,

24 Saying: What have we to do with thee, Jesus of Nazareth? art thou come to destroy us? I know who thou art, the Holy One of God.

25 And Jesus threatened him, saying: Speak no more, and go out of the man.

26 And the unclean spirit tearing him, and crying out with a loud voice, went out of him.

27 And they were all amazed, insomuch that they questioned among themselves, saying: What thing is this? what is this new doctrine? for with power he commandeth even the unclean spirits, and they obey him.

28 And the fame of him was spread forthwith into all the country of Galilee.

~

THURSDAY JANUARY 16, 2025

First Reading: Hebrews 3: 7-14

Responsorial Psalm: Psalms 95: 6-7c, 8-9, 10-11

Alleluia: Matthew 4: 23

Gospel: Mark 1: 40-45

First Reading: Hebrews 3: 7-14

7 Wherefore, as the Holy Ghost saith: Today if you shall hear his voice,

8 Harden not your hearts, as in the provocation; in the day of temptation in the desert,

9 Where your fathers tempted me, proved and saw my works,

10 Forty years: for which cause I was offended with this generation, and I said: They always err in heart. And they have not known my ways,

11 As I have sworn in my wrath: If they shall enter into my rest.

12 Take heed, brethren, lest perhaps there be in any of you an evil heart of unbelief, to depart from the living God.

13 But exhort one another every day, whilst it is called today, that none of you be hardened through the deceitfulness of sin.

14 For we are made partakers of Christ: yet so, if we hold the beginning of his substance firm unto the end.

Responsorial Psalm: Psalms 95: 6-7c, 8-9, 10-11

R. (8) If today you hear his voice, harden not your hearts.

6 Come let us adore and fall down: and weep before the Lord that made us.

7c For he is the Lord our God: and we are the people of his pasture and the sheep of his hand.

R. If today you hear his voice, harden not your hearts.

8 Today if you shall hear his voice, harden not your hearts:

9 As in the provocation, according to the day of temptation in the wilderness: where your fathers tempted me, they proved me, and saw my works.

R. If today you hear his voice, harden not your hearts.

10 Forty years long was I offended with that generation, and I said: These always err in heart.

11 And these men have not known my ways: so I swore in my wrath that they shall not enter into my rest.

R. If today you hear his voice, harden not your hearts.

Alleluia: Matthew 4: 23

R. Alleluia, alleluia.

23 Jesus preached the Gospel of the Kingdom and cured every disease among the people.

R. Alleluia, alleluia.

Gospel: Mark 1: 40-45

40 And there came a leper to him, beseeching him, and kneeling down said to him: If thou wilt, thou canst make me clean.

41 And Jesus having compassion on him, stretched forth his hand; and touching him, saith to him: I will. Be thou made clean.

42 And when he had spoken, immediately the leprosy departed from him, and he was made clean.

43 And he strictly charged him, and forthwith sent him away.

44 And he saith to him: See thou tell no one; but go, shew thyself to the high priest, and offer for thy cleansing the things that Moses commanded, for a testimony to them.

45 But he being gone out, began to publish and to blaze abroad the word: so that he could not openly go into the city, but was without in desert places: and they flocked to him from all sides.

~

FRIDAY JANUARY 17, 2025

First Reading: Hebrews 4: 1-5, 11

Responsorial Psalm: Psalms 78: 3 and 4bc, 6c-7, 8

Alleluia: Luke 7: 16

Gospel: Mark 2: 1-12

First Reading: Hebrews 4: 1-5, 11

1 Let us fear therefore lest the promise being left of entering into his rest, any of you should be thought to be wanting.

2 For unto us also it hath been declared, in like manner as unto them. But the word of hearing did not profit them, not being mixed with faith of those things they heard.

3 For we, who have believed, shall enter into rest; as he said: As I have sworn in my wrath; If they shall enter into my rest; and this indeed when the works from the foundation of the world were finished.

4 For in a certain place he spoke of the seventh day thus: And God rested the seventh day from all his works.

5 And in this place again: If they shall enter into my rest.

11 Let us hasten therefore to enter into that rest; lest any man fall into the same example of unbelief.

Responsorial Psalm: Psalms 78: 3 and 4bc, 6c-7, 8

R. (7b) Do not forget the works of the Lord!

3 How great things have we heard and known, and our fathers have told us.

4bc They have not been hidden from their children, in another generation. Declaring the praises of the Lord, and his powers, and his wonders which he hath done.

R. Do not forget the works of the Lord!

6c The children that should be born and should rise up, and declare them to their children.

7 That they may put their hope in God and may not forget the works of God: and may seek his commandments.

R. Do not forget the works of the Lord!

8 That they may not become like their fathers, a perverse and exasperating generation. A generation that set not their heart aright: and whose spirit was not faithful to God.

R. Do not forget the works of the Lord!

Alleluia: Luke 7: 16

R. Alleluia, alleluia.

16 A great prophet has arisen in our midst and God has visited his people.

R. Alleluia, alleluia.

Gospel: Mark 2: 1-12

1 And again he entered into Capharnaum after some days.

2 And it was heard that he was in the house, and many came together, so that there was no room; no, not even at the door; and he spoke to them the word.

3 And they came to him, bringing one sick of the palsy, who was carried by four.

4 And when they could not offer him unto him for the multitude, they uncovered the roof where he was; and opening it, they let down the bed wherein the man sick of the palsy lay.

5 And when Jesus had seen their faith, he saith to the sick of the palsy: Son, thy sins are forgiven thee.

6 And there were some of the scribes sitting there, and thinking in their hearts:

7 Why doth this man speak thus? he blasphemeth. Who can forgive sins, but God only?

8 Which Jesus presently knowing in his spirit, that they so thought within themselves, saith to them: Why think you these things in your hearts?

9 Which is easier, to say to the sick of the palsy: Thy sins are forgiven thee; or to say: Arise, take up thy bed, and walk?

10 But that you may know that the Son of man hath power on earth to forgive sins, (he saith to the sick of the palsy,)

11 I say to thee: Arise, take up thy bed, and go into thy house.

12 And immediately he arose; and taking up his bed, went his way in the sight of all; so that all wondered and glorified God, saying: We never saw the like.

～

SATURDAY JANUARY 18, 2025

First Reading: Hebrews 4: 12-16

Responsorial Psalm: Psalms 19: 8, 9, 10, 15

Alleluia: Luke 4: 18

Gospel: Mark 2: 13-17

First Reading: Hebrews 4: 12-16

12 For the word of God is living and effectual, and more piercing than any two edged sword; and reaching unto the division of the soul and the spirit, of the joints also and the marrow, and is a discerner of the thoughts and intents of the heart.

13 Neither is there any creature invisible in his sight: but all things are naked and open to his eyes, to whom our speech is.

14 Having therefore a great high priest that hath passed into the heavens, Jesus the Son of God: let us hold fast our confession.

15 For we have not a high priest, who can not have compassion on our infirmities: but one tempted in all things like as we are, without sin.

16 Let us go therefore with confidence to the throne of grace: that we may obtain mercy, and find grace in seasonable aid.

Responsorial Psalm: Psalms 19: 8, 9, 10, 15

R. (John 6:63c) Your words, Lord, are Spirit and life.

8 The law of the Lord is unspotted, converting souls: the testimony of the Lord is faithful, giving wisdom to little ones.

R. Your words, Lord, are Spirit and life.

9 The justices of the Lord are right, rejoicing hearts: the commandment of the Lord is lightsome, enlightening the eyes.

R. Your words, Lord, are Spirit and life.

10 The fear of the Lord is holy, enduring for ever and ever: the judgments of the Lord are true, justified in themselves.

R. Your words, Lord, are Spirit and life.

15 And the words of my mouth shall be such as may please: and the meditation of my heart always in thy sight. O Lord, my helper, and my redeemer.

R. Your words, Lord, are Spirit and life.

Alleluia: Luke 4: 18

R. Alleluia, alleluia.

18 The Lord sent me to bring glad tidings to the poor and to proclaim liberty to captives.

R. Alleluia, alleluia.

Gospel: Mark 2: 13-17

13 And he went forth again to the sea side; and all the multitude came to him, and he taught them.

14 And when he was passing by, he saw Levi the son of Alpheus sitting at the receipt of custom; and he saith to him: Follow me. And rising up, he followed him.

15 And it came to pass, that as he sat at meat in his house, many publicans and sinners sat down together with Jesus and his disciples. For they were many, who also followed him.

16 And the scribes and the Pharisees, seeing that he ate with publicans and sinners, said to his disciples: Why doth your master eat and drink with publicans and sinners?

17 Jesus hearing this, saith to them: They that are well have no need of a physician, but they that are sick. For I came not to call the just, but sinners.

SUNDAY JANUARY 19, 2025

First Reading: Isaiah 62: 1-5

Responsorial Psalm: Psalms 96: 1-2a, 2b-3, 7-8, 9-10

Second Reading: First Corinthians 12: 4-11

Alleluia: Second Thessalonians 2: 14

Gospel: John 2: 1-11

First Reading: Isaiah 62: 1-5

1 For Sion's sake I will not hold my peace, and for the sake of Jerusalem, I will not rest till her just one come forth as brightness, and her saviour be lighted as a lamp.

2 And the Gentiles shall see thy just one, and all kings thy glorious one: and thou shalt be called by a new name, which the mouth of the Lord shall name.

3 And thou shalt be a crown of glory in the hand of the Lord, and a royal diadem in the hand of thy God.

4 Thou shalt no more be called Forsaken: and thy land shall no more be called Desolate: but thou shalt be called My pleasure in her, and thy land inhabited. Because the Lord hath been well pleased with thee: and thy land shall be inhabited.

5 For the young man shall dwell with the virgin, and thy children shall dwell in thee. And the bridegroom shall rejoice over the bride, and thy God shall rejoice over thee.

Responsorial Psalm: Psalms 96: 1-2a, 2b-3, 7-8, 9-10

R. (3) Proclaim his marvelous deeds to all the nations.

1 Sing ye to the Lord a new canticle: sing to the Lord, all the earth.

2a Sing ye to the Lord and bless his name.

R. Proclaim his marvelous deeds to all the nations.

2b Shew forth his salvation from day to day.

3 Declare his glory among the Gentiles: his wonders among all people.

R. Proclaim his marvelous deeds to all the nations.

7 Bring ye to the Lord, O ye kindreds of the Gentiles, bring ye to the Lord glory and honour:

8 Bring to the Lord glory unto his name. Bring up sacrifices, and come into his courts:

R. Proclaim his marvelous deeds to all the nations.

9 Adore ye the Lord in his holy court. Let all the earth be moved at his presence.

10 Say ye among the Gentiles, the Lord hath reigned. For he hath corrected the world, which shall not be moved: he will judge the people with justice.

R. Proclaim his marvelous deeds to all the nations.

Second Reading: First Corinthians 12: 4-11

4 Now there are diversities of graces, but the same Spirit;

5 And there are diversities of ministries, but the same Lord;

6 And there are diversities of operations, but the same God, who worketh all in all.

7 And the manifestation of the Spirit is given to every man unto profit.

8 To one indeed, by the Spirit, is given the word of wisdom: and to another, the word of knowledge, according to the same Spirit;

9 To another, faith in the same spirit; to another, the grace of healing in one Spirit;

10 To another, the working of miracles; to another, prophecy; to another, the discerning of spirits; to another, diverse kinds of tongues; to another, interpretation of speeches.

11 But all these things one and the same Spirit worketh, dividing to every one according as he will.

Alleluia: Second Thessalonians 2: 14

R. Alleluia, alleluia.

14 God has called us through the Gospel to possess the glory of our Lord Jesus Christ.

R. Alleluia, alleluia.

Gospel: John 2: 1-11

1 And the third day, there was a marriage in Cana of Galilee: and the mother of Jesus was there.

2 And Jesus also was invited, and his diswater potsciples, to the marriage.

3 And the wine failing, the mother of Jesus saith to him: They have no wine.

4 And Jesus saith to her: Woman, what is that to me and to thee? my hour is not yet come.

5 His mother saith to the waiters: Whatsoever he shall say to you, do ye.

6 Now there were set there six water pots of stone, according to the manner of the purifying of the Jews, containing two or three measures apiece.

7 Jesus saith to them: Fill the water pots with water. And they filled them up to the brim.

8 And Jesus saith to them: Draw out now, and carry to the chief steward of the feast. And they carried it.

9 And when the chief steward had tasted the water made wine, and knew not whence it was, but the waiters knew who had drawn the water; the chief steward calleth the bridegroom,

10 And saith to him: Every man at first setteth forth good wine, and when men have well drunk, then that which is worse. But thou hast kept the good wine until now.

11 This beginning of miracles did Jesus in Cana of Galilee; and manifested his glory, and his disciples believed in him.

∼

MONDAY JANUARY 20, 2025

First Reading: Hebrews 5: 1-10

Responsorial Psalm: Psalms 110: 1, 2, 3, 4

Alleluia: Hebrews 4: 12

Gospel: Mark 2: 18-22

First Reading: Hebrews 5: 1-10

1 For every high priest taken from among men, is ordained for men in the things that appertain to God, that he may offer up gifts and sacrifices for sins:

2 Who can have compassion on them that are ignorant and that err: because he himself also is compassed with infirmity.

3 And therefore he ought, as for the people, so also for himself, to offer for sins.

4 Neither doth any man take the honour to himself, but he that is called by God, as Aaron was.

5 So Christ also did not glorify himself, that he might be made a high priest: but he that said unto him: Thou art my Son, this day have I begotten thee.

6 As he saith also in another place: Thou art a priest for ever, according to the order of Melchisedech.

7 Who in the days of his flesh, with a strong cry and tears, offering up prayers and supplications to him that was able to save him from death, was heard for his reverence.

8 And whereas indeed he was the Son of God, he learned obedience by the things which he suffered:

9 And being consummated, he became, to all that obey him, the cause of eternal salvation.

10 Called by God a high priest according to the order of Melchisedech.

Responsorial Psalm: Psalms 110: 1, 2, 3, 4

R. (4b) You are a priest for ever, in the line of Melchizedek.

1 The Lord said to my Lord: Sit thou at my right hand: Until I make thy enemies thy footstool.

R. You are a priest for ever, in the line of Melchizedek.

2 The Lord will send forth the sceptre of thy power out of Sion: rule thou in the midst of thy enemies.

R. You are a priest for ever, in the line of Melchizedek.

3 With thee is the principality in the day of thy strength: in the brightness of the saints: from the womb before the day star I begot thee.

R. You are a priest for ever, in the line of Melchizedek.

4 The Lord hath sworn, and he will not repent: Thou art a priest for ever according to the order of Melchisedech.

R. You are a priest for ever, in the line of Melchizedek.

Alleluia: Hebrews 4: 12

R. Alleluia, alleluia.

12 The word of God is living and effective, able to discern reflections and thoughts of the heart.

R. Alleluia, alleluia.

Gospel: Mark 2: 18-22

18 And the disciples of John and the Pharisees used to fast; and they come and say to him: Why do the disciples of John and of the Pharisees fast; but thy disciples do not fast?

19 And Jesus saith to them: Can the children of the marriage fast, as long as the bridegroom is with them? As long as they have the bridegroom with them, they cannot fast.

20 But the days will come when the bridegroom shall be taken away from them; and then they shall fast in those days.

21 No man seweth a piece of raw cloth to an old garment: otherwise the new piecing taketh away from the old, and there is made a greater rent.

22 And no man putteth new wine into old bottles: otherwise the wine will burst the bottles, and both the wine will be spilled, and the bottles will be lost. But new wine must be put into new bottles.

❧

TUESDAY JANUARY 21, 2025

First Reading: Hebrews 6: 10-20

Responsorial Psalm: Psalms 111: 1-2, 4-5, 9 and 10c

Alleluia: Ephesians 1: 17-18

Gospel: Mark 2: 23-28

First Reading: Hebrews 6: 10-20

10 For God is not unjust, that he should forget your work, and the love which you have shewn in his name, you who have ministered, and do minister to the saints.

11 And we desire that every one of you shew forth the same carefulness to the accomplishing of hope unto the end:

12 That you become not slothful, but followers of them, who through faith and patience shall inherit the promises.

13 For God making promise to Abraham, because he had no one greater by whom he might swear, swore by himself,

14 Saying: Unless blessing I shall bless thee, and multiplying I shall multiply thee.

15 And so patiently enduring he obtained the promise.

16 For men swear by one greater than themselves: and an oath for confirmation is the end of all their controversy.

17 Wherein God, meaning more abundantly to shew to the heirs of the promise the immutability of his counsel, interposed an oath:

18 That by two immutable things, in which it is impossible for God to lie, we may have the strongest comfort, who have fled for refuge to hold fast the hope set before us.

19 Which we have as an anchor of the soul, sure and firm, and which entereth in even within the veil;

20 Where the forerunner Jesus is entered for us, made a high priest for ever according to the order of Melchisedech.

Responsorial Psalm: Psalms 111: 1-2, 4-5, 9 and 10c

144

R. (5) The Lord will remember his covenant for ever.

or

R. Alleluia.

1 I will praise thee, O Lord, with my whole heart; in the council of the just: and in the congregation.

2 Great are the works of the Lord: sought out according to all his wills.

R. The Lord will remember his covenant for ever.

or

R. Alleluia.

4 He hath made a remembrance of his wonderful works, being a merciful and gracious Lord:

5 He hath given food to them that fear him. He will be mindful for ever of his covenant:

R. The Lord will remember his covenant for ever.

or

R. Alleluia.

9 He hath sent redemption to his people: he hath commanded his covenant for ever. Holy and terrible is his name:

10c His praise continueth for ever and ever.

R. The Lord will remember his covenant for ever.

or

R. Alleluia.

Alleluia: Ephesians 1: 17-18

R. Alleluia, alleluia.

17-18 May the Father of our Lord Jesus Christ enlighten the eyes of our hearts, that we may know what is the hope that belongs to our call.

R. Alleluia, alleluia.

Gospel: Mark 2: 23-28

23 And it came to pass again, as the Lord walked through the corn fields on the sabbath, that his disciples began to go forward, and to pluck the ears of corn.

24 And the Pharisees said to him: Behold, why do they on the sabbath day that which is not lawful?

25 And he said to them: Have you never read what David did when he had need, and was hungry himself, and they that were with him?

26 How he went into the house of God, under Abiathar the high priest, and did eat the loaves of proposition, which was not lawful to eat but for the priests, and gave to them who were with him?

27 And he said to them: The sabbath was made for man, and not man for the sabbath.

28 Therefore the Son of man is Lord of the sabbath also.

~

WEDNESDAY JANUARY 22, 2025

First Reading: Hebrews 7: 1-3, 15-17

Responsorial Psalm: Psalms 110: 1, 2, 3, 4

Alleluia: Matthew 4: 23

Gospel: Mark 3: 1-6

First Reading: Hebrews 7: 1-3, 15-17

1 For this Melchisedech was king of Salem, priest of the most high God, who met Abraham returning from the slaughter of the kings, and blessed him:

2 To whom also Abraham divided the tithes of all: who first indeed by interpretation, is king of justice: and then also king of Salem, that is, king of peace:

3 Without father, without mother, without genealogy, having neither beginning of days nor end of life, but likened unto the Son of God, continueth a priest for ever.

15 And it is yet far more evident: if according to the similitude of Melchisedech there ariseth another priest,

16 Who is made not according to the law of a carnal commandment, but according to the power of an indissoluble life:

17 For he testifieth: Thou art a priest for ever, according to the order of Melchisedech.

Responsorial Psalm: Psalms 110: 1, 2, 3, 4

R. (4b) You are a priest for ever, in the line of Melchizedek.

1 The Lord said to my Lord: Sit thou at my right hand: Until I make thy enemies thy footstool.

R. You are a priest for ever, in the line of Melchizedek.

2 The Lord will send forth the sceptre of thy power out of Sion: rule thou in the midst of thy enemies.

R. You are a priest for ever, in the line of Melchizedek.

3 With thee is the principality in the day of thy strength: in the brightness of the saints: from the womb before the day star I begot thee.

R. You are a priest for ever, in the line of Melchizedek.

4 The Lord hath sworn, and he will not repent: Thou art a priest for ever according to the order of Melchisedech.

R. You are a priest for ever, in the line of Melchizedek.

Alleluia: Matthew 4: 23

R. Alleluia, alleluia.

23 Jesus preached the Gospel of the Kingdom and cured every disease among the people.

R. Alleluia, alleluia.

Gospel: Mark 3: 1-6

1 And he entered again into the synagogue, and there was a man there who had a withered hand.

2 And they watched him whether he would heal on the sabbath days; that they might accuse him.

3 And he said to the man who had the withered hand: Stand up in the midst.

4 And he saith to them: Is it lawful to do good on the sabbath days, or to do evil? to save life, or to destroy? But they held their peace.

5 And looking round about on them with anger, being grieved for the blindness of their hearts, he saith to the man: Stretch forth thy hand. And he stretched it forth: and his hand was restored unto him.

6 And the Pharisees going out, immediately made a consultation with the Herodians against him, how they might destroy him.

∽

THURSDAY JANUARY 23, 2025

First Reading: Hebrews 7: 25 – 8: 6

Responsorial Psalm: Psalms 40: 7-8a, 8b-9, 10, 17

Alleluia: Second Timothy 1: 10

Gospel: Mark 3: 7-12

First Reading: Hebrews 7: 25 – 8: 6

25 Whereby he is able also to save for ever them that come to God by him; always living to make intercession for us.

26 For it was fitting that we should have such a high priest, holy, innocent, undefiled, separated from sinners, and made higher than the heavens;

27 Who needeth not daily (as the other priests) to offer sacrifices first for his own sins, and then for the people's: for this he did once, in offering himself.

28 For the law maketh men priests, who have infirmity: but the word of the oath, which was since the law, the Son who is perfected for evermore.

8:1 Now of the things which we have spoken, this is the sum: We have such a high priest, who is set on the right hand of the throne of majesty in the heavens,

2 A minister of the holies, and of the true tabernacle, which the Lord hath pitched, and not man.

3 For every high priest is appointed to offer gifts and sacrifices: wherefore it is necessary that he also should have some thing to offer.

4 If then he were on earth, he would not be a priest: seeing that there would be others to offer gifts according to the law,

5 Who serve unto the example and shadow of heavenly things. As it was answered to Moses, when he was to finish the tabernacle: See (saith he) that thou make all things according to the pattern which was shewn thee on the mount.

6 But now he hath obtained a better ministry, by how much also he is a mediator of a better testament, which is established on better promises.

Responsorial Psalm: Psalms 40: 7-8a, 8b-9, 10, 17

R. (8a and 9a) Here am I, Lord; I come to do your will.

7 Sacrifice and oblation thou didst not desire; but thou hast pierced ears for me. Burnt offering and sin offering thou didst not require:

8a Then said I, Behold I come.

R. Here am I, Lord; I come to do your will.

8b In the head of the book it is written of me

9 That I should do thy will: O my God, I have desired it, and thy law in the midst of my heart.

R. Here am I, Lord; I come to do your will.

10 I have declared thy justice in a great church, lo, I will not restrain my lips: O Lord, thou knowest it.

R. Here am I, Lord; I come to do your will.

17 Let all that seek thee rejoice and be glad in thee: and let such as love thy salvation say always: The Lord be magnified.

R. Here am I, Lord; I come to do your will.

Alleluia: Second Timothy 1: 10

R. Alleluia, alleluia.

10 Our Savior Jesus Christ has destroyed death and brought life to light through the Gospel.

R. Alleluia, alleluia.

Gospel: Mark 3: 7-12

7 But Jesus retired with his disciples to the sea; and a great multitude followed him from Galilee and Judea,

8 And from Jerusalem, and from Idumea, and from beyond the Jordan. And they about Tyre and Sidon, a great multitude, hearing the things which he did, came to him.

9 And he spoke to his disciples that a small ship should wait on him because of the multitude, lest they should throng him.

10 For he healed many, so that they pressed upon him for to touch him, as many as had evils.

11 And the unclean spirits, when they saw him, fell down before him: and they cried, saying:

12 Thou art the Son of God. And he strictly charged them that they should not make him known.

~

FRIDAY JANUARY 24, 2025

First Reading: Hebrews 8: 6-13

Responsorial Psalm: Psalms 85: 8 and 10, 11-12, 13-14

Gospel: Mark 3: 13-19

First Reading: Hebrews 8: 6-13

6 But now he hath obtained a better ministry, by how much also he is a mediator of a better testament, which is established on better promises.

7 For if that former had been faultless, there should not indeed a place have been sought for a second.

8 For finding fault with them, he saith: Behold, the days shall come, saith the Lord: and I will perfect unto the house of Israel, and unto the house of Juda, a new testament:

9 Not according to the testament which I made to their fathers, on the day when I took them by the hand to lead them out of the land of Egypt: because they continued not in my testament: and I regarded them not, saith the Lord.

10 For this is the testament which I will make to the house of Israel after those days, saith the Lord: I will give my laws into their mind, and in their heart will I write them: and I will be their God, and they shall be my people:

11 And they shall not teach every man his neighbour and every man his brother, saying, Know the Lord: for all shall know me from the least to the greatest of them:

12 Because I will be merciful to their iniquities, and their sins I will remember no more.

13 Now in saying a new, he hath made the former old. And that which decayeth and groweth old, is near its end.

Responsorial Psalm: Psalms 85: 8 and 10, 11-12, 13-14

R. (11a) Kindness and truth shall meet.

8 Shew us, O Lord, thy mercy; and grant us thy salvation.

10 Surely his salvation is near to them that fear him: that glory may dwell in our land.

R. Kindness and truth shall meet.

11 Mercy and truth have met each other: justice and peace have kissed.

12 Truth is sprung out of the earth: and justice hath looked down from heaven.

R. Kindness and truth shall meet.

13 For the Lord will give goodness: and our earth shall yield her fruit.

14 Justice shall walk before him: and shall set his steps in the way.

R. Kindness and truth shall meet.

Alleluia

R. Alleluia, alleluia.

God was reconciling the world to himself in Christ, and entrusting to us the message of reconciliation.

R. Alleluia, alleluia.

Gospel: Mark 3: 13-19

13 And going up into a mountain, he called unto him whom he would himself: and they came to him.

14 And he made that twelve should be with him, and that he might send them to preach.

15 And he gave them power to heal sicknesses, and to cast out devils.

16 And to Simon he gave the name Peter:

17 And James the son of Zebedee, and John the brother of James; and he named them Boanerges, which is, The sons of thunder:

18 And Andrew and Philip, and Bartholomew and Matthew, and Thomas and James of Alpheus, and Thaddeus, and Simon the Cananean:

19 And Judas Iscariot, who also betrayed him.

❧

SATURDAY JANUARY 25, 2025

First Reading: Acts 22: 3-16 or Acts 9: 1-22

Responsorial Psalm: Psalms 117: 1bc, 2

Alleluia: John 15: 16

Gospel: Mark 16: 15-18

First Reading: Acts 22: 3-16 or Acts 9: 1-22

Acts 22: 3-16

3 And he saith: I am a Jew, born at Tarsus in Cilicia, but brought up in this city, at the feet of Gamaliel, taught according to the truth of the law of the fathers, zealous for the law, as also all you are this day:

4 Who persecuted this way unto death, binding and delivering into prisons both men and women.

5 As the high priest doth bear me witness, and all the ancients: from whom also receiving letters to the brethren, I went to Damascus, that I might bring them bound from thence to Jerusalem to be punished.

6 And it came to pass, as I was going, and drawing nigh to Damascus at midday, that suddenly from heaven there shone round about me a great light:

7 And falling on the ground, I heard a voice saying to me: Saul, Saul, why persecutest thou me?

8 And I answered: Who art thou, Lord? And he said to me: I am Jesus of Nazareth, whom thou persecutest.

9 And they that were with me, saw indeed the light, but they heard not the voice of him that spoke with me.

10 And I said: What shall I do, Lord? And the Lord said to me: Arise, and go to Damascus; and there it shall be told thee of all things that thou must do.

11 And whereas I did not see for the brightness of that light, being led by the hand by my companions, I came to Damascus.

12 And one Ananias, a man according to the law, having testimony of all the Jews who dwelt there,

13 Coming to me, and standing by me, said to me: Brother Saul, look up. And I the same hour looked upon him.

14 But he said: The God of our fathers hath preordained thee that thou shouldst know his will, and see the Just One, and shouldst hear the voice from his mouth.

15 For thou shalt be his witness to all men, of those things which thou hast seen and heard.

16 And now why tarriest thou? Rise up, and be baptized, and wash away thy sins, invoking his name.

Acts 9: 1-22

1 And Saul, as yet breathing out threatenings and slaughter against the disciples of the Lord, went to the high priest,

2 And asked of him letters to Damascus, to the synagogues: that if he found any men and women of this way, he might bring them bound to Jerusalem.

3 And as he went on his journey, it came to pass that he drew nigh to Damascus; and suddenly a light from heaven shined round about him.

4 And falling on the ground, he heard a voice saying to him: Saul, Saul, why persecutest thou me?

5 Who said: Who art thou, Lord? And he: I am Jesus whom thou persecutest. It is hard for thee to kick against the goad.

6 And he trembling and astonished, said: Lord, what wilt thou have me to do?

7 And the Lord said to him: Arise, and go into the city, and there it shall be told thee what thou must do. Now the men who went in company with him, stood amazed, hearing indeed a voice, but seeing no man.

8 And Saul arose from the ground; and when his eyes were opened, he saw nothing. But they leading him by the hands, brought him to Damascus.

9 And he was there three days, without sight, and he did neither eat nor drink.

10 Now there was a certain disciple at Damascus, named Ananias. And the Lord said to him in a vision: Ananias. And he said: Behold I am here, Lord.

11 And the Lord said to him: Arise, and go into the street that is called Straight, and seek in the house of Judas, one named Saul of Tarsus. For behold he prayeth.

12 (And he saw a man named Ananias coming in, and putting his hands upon him, that he might receive his sight.)

13 But Ananias answered: Lord, I have heard by many of this man, how much evil he hath done to thy saints in Jerusalem.

14 And here he hath authority from the chief priests to bind all that invoke thy name.

15 And the Lord said to him: Go thy way; for this man is to me a vessel of election, to carry my name before the Gentiles, and kings, and the children of Israel.

16 For I will shew him how great things he must suffer for my name's sake.

17 And Ananias went his way, and entered into the house. And laying his hands upon him, he said: Brother Saul, the Lord Jesus hath sent me, he that

appeared to thee in the way as thou camest; that thou mayest receive thy sight, and be filled with the Holy Ghost.

18 And immediately there fell from his eyes as it were scales, and he received his sight; and rising up, he was baptized.

19 And when he had taken meat, he was strengthened. And he was with the disciples that were at Damascus, for some days.

20 And immediately he preached Jesus in the synagogues, that he is the Son of God.

21 And all that heard him, were astonished, and said: Is not this he who perse-cuted in Jerusalem those that called upon this name: and came hither for that intent, that he might carry them bound to the chief priests?

22 But Saul increased much more in strength, and confounded the Jews who dwelt at Damascus, affirming that this is the Christ.

Responsorial Psalm: Psalms 117: 1bc, 2

R. (mark 16:15) Go out to all the world, and tell the Good News.

or

R. Alleluia.

1bc O praise the Lord, all ye nations: praise him, all ye people.

R. Go out to all the world, and tell the Good News.

or

R. Alleluia.

2 For his mercy is confirmed upon us: and the truth of the Lord remaineth for ever.

R. Go out to all the world, and tell the Good News.

or

R. Alleluia.

Alleluia: John 15: 16

R. Alleluia, alleluia.

16 I chose you from the world, to go and bear fruit that will last, says the Lord.

R. Alleluia, alleluia.

Gospel: Mark 16: 15-18

15 And he said to them: Go ye into the whole world, and preach the gospel to every creature.

16 He that believeth and is baptized, shall be saved: but he that believeth not shall be condemned.

17 And these signs shall follow them that believe: In my name they shall cast out devils: they shall speak with new tongues.

18 They shall take up serpents; and if they shall drink any deadly thing, it shall not hurt them: they shall lay their hands upon the sick, and they shall recover.

～

SUNDAY JANUARY 26, 2025

First Reading: Nehemiah 8: 2-4a, 5-6, 8-10

Responsorial Psalm: Psalms 19: 8, 9, 10, 15

Second Reading: First Corinthians 12: 12-30 or First Corinthians 12: 12-14, 27

Alleluia: Luke 4: 18

Gospel: Luke 1: 1-4; 4: 14-21

―――――――――――

First Reading: Nehemiah 8: 2-4a, 5-6, 8-10

2 Then **Esdras** the priest brought the law before the multitude of men and women, and all those that could understand, in the first day of the seventh month.

3 And he read it plainly in the street that was before the water gate, from the morning until midday, before the men, and the women, and all those that could understand: and the ears of all the people were attentive to the book.

4a And **Esdras** the scribe stood upon a step of wood, which he had made to speak upon.

5 And **Esdras** opened the book before all the people: for he was above all the people: and when he had opened it, all the people stood.

6 And **Esdras** blessed the Lord the great God: and all the people answered, Amen, amen: lifting up their hands: and they bowed down, and adored God with their faces to the ground.

8 And they read in the book of the law of God distinctly and plainly to be understood: and they understood when it was read.

9 And **Nehemias** (he is **Athersatha**) and **Esdras** the priest and scribe, and the Levites who interpreted to all the people, said: This is a holy day to the Lord our God: do not mourn, nor weep: for all the people wept, when they heard the words of the law.

10 And he said to them: Go, eat fat meats, and drink sweet wine, and send portions to them that have not prepared for themselves: because it is the holy day of the Lord, and be not sad: for the joy of the Lord is our strength.

Responsorial Psalm: Psalms 19: 8, 9, 10, 15

R. (John 6:63c) Your words, Lord, are Spirit and life.

8 The law of the Lord is unspotted, converting souls: the testimony of the Lord is faithful, giving wisdom to little ones.

R. Your words, Lord, are Spirit and life.

9 The justices of the Lord are right, rejoicing hearts: the commandment of the Lord is lightsome, enlightening the eyes.

R. Your words, Lord, are Spirit and life.

10 The fear of the Lord is holy, enduring for ever and ever: the judgments of the Lord are true, justified in themselves.

R. Your words, Lord, are Spirit and life.

15 And the words of my mouth shall be such as may please: and the meditation of my heart always in thy sight. O Lord, my helper, and my redeemer.

R. Your words, Lord, are Spirit and life.

Second Reading: First Corinthians 12: 12-30 or First Corinthians 12: 12-14, 27

12 For as the body is one, and hath many members; and all the members of the body, whereas they are many, yet are one body, so also is Christ.

13 For in one Spirit were we all baptized into one body, whether Jews or Gentiles, whether bond or free; and in one Spirit we have all been made to drink.

14 For the body also is not one member, but many.

15 If the foot should say, because I am not the hand, I am not of the body; is it therefore not of the body?

16 And if the ear should say, because I am not the eye, I am not of the body; is it therefore not of the body?

17 If the whole body were the eye, where would be the hearing? If the whole were hearing, where would be the smelling?

18 But now God hath set the members every one of them in the body as it hath pleased him.

19 And if they all were one member, where would be the body?

20 But now there are many members indeed, yet one body.

21 And the eye cannot say to the hand: I need not thy help; nor again the head to the feet: I have no need of you.

22 Yea, much more those that seem to be the more feeble members of the body, are more necessary.

23 And such as we think to be the less honourable members of the body, about these we put more abundant honour; and those that are our uncomely parts, have more abundant comeliness.

24 But our comely parts have no need: but God hath tempered the body together, giving to that which wanted the more abundant honour,

25 That there might be no schism in the body; but the members might be mutually careful one for another.

26 And if one member suffer any thing, all the members suffer with it; or if one member glory, all the members rejoice with it.

27 Now you are the body of Christ, and members of member.

28 And God indeed hath set some in the church; first apostles, secondly

prophets, thirdly doctors; after that miracles; then the graces of healing, helps, governments, kinds of tongues, interpretations of speeches.

29 Are all apostles? Are all prophets? Are all doctors?

30 Are all workers of miracles? Have all the grace of healing? Do all speak with tongues? Do all interpret?

Alleluia: Luke 4: 18

R. Alleluia, alleluia.

18 The Lord sent me to bring glad tidings to the poor, and to proclaim liberty to captives.

R. Alleluia, alleluia.

Gospel: Luke 1: 1-4; 4: 14-21

1 Forasmuch as many have taken in hand to set forth in order a narration of the things that have been accomplished among us;

2 According as they have delivered them unto us, who from the beginning were eyewitnesses and ministers of the word:

3 It seemed good to me also, having diligently attained to all things from the beginning, to write to thee in order, most excellent **Theophilus,**

4 That thou mayest know the verity of those words in which thou hast been instructed.

4:14 And **Jesus** returned in the power of the spirit, into Galilee, and the fame of him went out through the whole country.

15 And he taught in their synagogues, and was magnified by all.

16 And he came to **Nazareth,** where he was brought up: and he went into the synagogue, according to his custom, on the sabbath day; and he rose up to read.

17 And the book of **Isaias** the prophet was delivered unto him. And as he unfolded the book, he found the place where it was written:

18 The Spirit of the Lord is upon me. Wherefore he hath anointed me to preach the gospel to the poor, he hath sent me to heal the contrite of heart,

19 To preach deliverance to the captives, and sight to the blind, to set at

liberty them that are bruised, to preach the acceptable year of the Lord, and the day of reward.

20 And when he had folded the book, he restored it to the minister, and sat down. And the eyes of all in the synagogue were fixed on him.

21 And he began to say to them: This day is fulfilled this scripture in your ears.

∿

MONDAY JANUARY 27, 2025

First Reading: Hebrews 9: 15, 24-28

Responsorial Psalm: Psalms 98: 1, 2-3ab, 3cd-4, 5-6

Alleluia: Second Timothy 1: 10

Gospel: Mark 3: 22-30

First Reading: Hebrews 9: 15, 24-28

15 And therefore he is the **mediator** of the new testament: that by means of his death, for the redemption of those transgressions, which were under the former testament, they that are called may receive the promise of eternal inheritance.

24 For **Jesus** is not entered into the holies made with hands, the patterns of the true: but into heaven itself, that he may appear now in the presence of **God** for us.

25 Nor yet that he should offer himself often, as the high priest entereth into the holies, every year with the blood of others:

26 For then he ought to have suffered often from the beginning of the world: but now once at the end of ages, he hath appeared for the destruction of sin, by the sacrifice of himself.

27 And as it is appointed unto men once to die, and after this the judgment:

28 So also **Christ** was offered once to exhaust the sins of many; the second time he shall appear without sin to them that expect him unto salvation.

Responsorial Psalm: Psalms 98: 1, 2-3ab, 3cd-4, 5-6

R. (1a) Sing to the Lord a new song, for he has done marvelous deeds.

1 Sing ye to the Lord anew canticle: because he hath done wonderful things. His right hand hath wrought for him salvation, and his arm is holy.

R. Sing to the Lord a new song, for he has done marvelous deeds.

2 The Lord hath made known his salvation: he hath revealed his justice in the sight of the Gentiles.

3ab He hath remembered his mercy his truth toward the house of **Israel**.

R. Sing to the Lord a new song, for he has done marvelous deeds.

3cd All the ends of the earth have seen the salvation of our **God**.

4 Sing joyfully to **God**, all the earth; make melody, rejoice and sing.

R. Sing to the Lord a new song, for he has done marvelous deeds.

5 Sing praise to the Lord on the harp, on the harp, and with the voice of a psalm:

6 With long trumpets, and sound of comet. Make a joyful noise before the Lord our **king**:

R. Sing to the Lord a new song, for he has done marvelous deeds.

Alleluia: Second Timothy 1: 10

R. Alleluia, alleluia.

10 Our **Savior Jesus Christ** has destroyed death and brought life to light through the **Gospel**.

R. Alleluia, alleluia.

Gospel: Mark 3: 22-30

22 And the scribes who were come down from **Jerusalem**, said: He hath **Beelzebub**, and by the prince of devils he casteth out devils.

23 And after he had called them together, he said to them in parables: How can **Satan** cast out **Satan**?

24 And if a kingdom be divided against itself, that kingdom cannot stand.

25 And if a house be divided against itself, that house cannot stand.

26 And if **Satan** be risen up against himself, he is divided, and cannot stand, but hath an end.

27 No man can enter into the house of a strong man and rob him of his goods, unless he first bind the strong man, and then shall he plunder his house.

28 Amen I say to you, that all sins shall be forgiven unto the sons of men, and the blasphemies wherewith they shall blaspheme:

29 But he that shall blaspheme against the **Holy Ghost**, shall never have forgiveness, but shall be guilty of an everlasting sin.

30 Because they said: He hath an unclean spirit.

TUESDAY JANUARY 28, 2025

First Reading: Hebrews 10: 1-10

Responsorial Psalm: Psalms 40: 2 and 4ab, 7-8a, 10, 11

Alleluia: Matthew 11: 25

Gospel: Mark 3: 31-35

First Reading: Hebrews 10: 1-10

1 For the **law** having a shadow of the good things to come, not the very image of the things; by the selfsame sacrifices which they offer continually every year, can never make the comers thereunto perfect:

2 For then they would have ceased to be offered: because the worshippers once cleansed should have no conscience of sin any longer:

3 But in them there is made a commemoration of sins every year.

4 For it is impossible that with the blood of oxen and goats sin should be taken away.

5 Wherefore when he cometh into the world, he saith: Sacrifice and oblation thou wouldest not: but a body thou hast fitted to me:

6 Holocausts for sin did not please thee.

7 Then said I: Behold I come: in the head of the book it is written of me: that I should do thy will, O **God**.

8 In saying before, Sacrifices, and oblations, and holocausts for sin thou wouldest not, neither are they pleasing to thee, which are offered according to the **law**.

9 Then said I: Behold, I come to do thy will, O **God**: he taketh away the first, that he may establish that which followeth.

10 In the which will, we are sanctified by the oblation of the body of **Jesus Christ** once.

Responsorial Psalm: Psalms 40: 2 and 4ab, 7-8a, 10, 11

R. (8a and 9a) Here am I **Lord**; I come to do your will.

2 With expectation I have waited for the **Lord**, and he was attentive to me.

4ab And he put a new canticle into my mouth, a song to our **God**.

R. Here am I **Lord**; I come to do your will.

7 Sacrifice and oblation thou didst not desire; but thou hast pierced ears for me. Burnt offering and sin offering thou didst not require:

8a Then said I, Behold I come.

R. Here am I **Lord**; I come to do your will.

10 I have declared thy justice in a great church, lo, I will not restrain my lips: O **Lord**, thou knowest it.

R. Here am I **Lord**; I come to do your will.

11 I have not hid thy justice within my heart: I have declared thy truth and thy salvation. I have not concealed thy mercy and thy truth from a great council.

R. Here am I **Lord**; I come to do your will.

Alleluia: Matthew 11: 25

R. Alleluia, alleluia.

25 Blessed are you, **Father**, **Lord** of heaven and earth; you have revealed to little ones the mysteries of the **Kingdom**.

R. Alleluia, alleluia.

Gospel: Mark 3: 31-35

31 And his **mother** and his **brethren** came; and standing without, sent unto him, calling him.

32 And the multitude sat about him; and they say to him: Behold thy **mother** and thy **brethren** without seek for thee.

33 And answering them, he said: Who is my **mother** and my **brethren**?

34 And looking round about on them who sat about him, he saith: Behold my **mother** and my **brethren**.

35 For whosoever shall do the will of **God**, he is my **brother**, and my **sister**, and **mother**.

~

WEDNESDAY JANUARY 29, 2025

First Reading: Hebrews 10: 11-18

Responsorial Psalm: Psalms 110: 1, 2, 3, 4

Gospel: Mark 4: 1-20

First Reading: Hebrews 10: 11-18

11 And every **priest** indeed standeth daily ministering, and often offering the same sacrifices, which can never take away sins.

12 But this man offering one sacrifice for sins, for ever sitteth on the right hand of **God**,

13 From henceforth expecting, until his enemies be made his footstool.

14 For by one oblation he hath perfected for ever them that are sanctified.

15 And the **Holy Ghost** also doth testify this to us. For after that he said:

16 And this is the testament which I will make unto them after those days, saith the **Lord**. I will give my laws in their hearts, and on their minds will I write them:

17 And their sins and iniquities I will remember no more.

18 Now where there is a remission of these, there is no more an oblation for sin.

Responsorial Psalm: Psalms 110: 1, 2, 3, 4

R. (4b) You are a **priest** for ever, in the line of Melchizedek.

1 The **Lord** said to my **Lord**: Sit thou at my right hand: Until I make thy enemies thy footstool.

R. You are a **priest** for ever, in the line of Melchizedek.

2 The **Lord** will send forth the sceptre of thy power out of Sion: rule thou in the midst of thy enemies.

R. You are a **priest** for ever, in the line of Melchizedek.

3 With thee is the principality in the day of thy strength: in the brightness of the saints: from the womb before the day star I begot thee.

R. You are a **priest** for ever, in the line of Melchizedek.

4 The **Lord** hath sworn, and he will not repent: Thou art a **priest** for ever according to the order of Melchisedech.

R. You are a **priest** for ever, in the line of Melchizedek.

Alleluia

R. Alleluia, alleluia.

The seed is the **word** of **God, Christ** is the sower; all who come to him will live for ever.

R. Alleluia, alleluia.

Gospel: Mark 4: 1-20

1 And again he began to teach by the sea side; and a great multitude was gathered together unto him, so that he went up into a ship, and sat in the sea; and all the multitude was upon the land by the sea side.

2 And he taught them many things in parables, and said unto them in his doctrine:

3 Hear ye: Behold, the **sower** went out to sow.

4 And whilst he sowed, some fell by the way side, and the birds of the air came and ate it up.

5 And other some fell upon stony ground, where it had not much earth; and it shot up immediately, because it had no depth of earth.

6 And when the sun was risen, it was scorched; and because it had no root, it withered away.

7 And some fell among thorns; and the thorns grew up, and choked it, and it yielded no fruit.

8 And some fell upon good ground; and brought forth fruit that grew up, and increased and yielded, one thirty, another sixty, and another a hundred.

9 And he said: He that hath ears to hear, let him hear.

10 And when he was alone, the twelve that were with him asked him the parable.

11 And he said to them: To you it is given to know the mystery of the **kingdom** of **God**: but to them that are without, all things are done in parables:

12 That seeing they may see, and not perceive; and hearing they may hear, and not understand: lest at any time they should be converted, and their sins should be forgiven them.

13 And he saith to them: Are you ignorant of this parable? and how shall you know all parables?

14 He that soweth, soweth the **word**.

15 And these are they by the way side, where the **word** is sown, and as soon as they have heard, immediately Satan cometh and taketh away the **word** that was sown in their hearts.

16 And these likewise are they that are sown on the stony ground: who when they have heard the **word**, immediately receive it with joy.

17 And they have no root in themselves, but are only for a time: and then when tribulation and persecution ariseth for the **word** they are presently scandalized.

18 And others there are who are sown among thorns: these are they that hear the **word**,

19 And the cares of the world, and the deceitfulness of riches, and the lusts after other things entering in choke the **word**, and it is made fruitless.

20 And these are they who are sown upon the good ground, who hear the **word**, and receive it, and yield fruit, the one thirty, another sixty, and another a hundred.

~

THURSDAY JANUARY 30, 2025

First Reading: Hebrews 10: 19-25

Responsorial Psalm: Psalms 24: 1-2, 3-4ab, 5-6

Alleluia: Psalms 119: 105

Gospel: Mark 4: 21-25

First Reading: Hebrews 10: 19-25

19 Having therefore, brethren, a confidence in the entering into the **holies** by the **blood** of **Christ**;

20 A new and living way which he hath dedicated for us through the veil, that is to say, his **flesh**,

21 And a **high priest** over the house of **God**:

22 Let us draw near with a true heart in fulness of faith, having our hearts sprinkled from an evil conscience, and our bodies washed with clean water.

23 Let us hold fast the confession of our hope without wavering (for he is faithful that hath promised),

24 And let us consider one another, to provoke unto charity and to good works:

25 Not forsaking our assembly, as some are accustomed; but comforting one another, and so much the more as you see the day approaching.

Responsorial Psalm: Psalms 24: 1-2, 3-4ab, 5-6

R. (6) **Lord**, this is the people that longs to see your face.

1 The earth is the **Lord's** and the fulness thereof: the world, and all they that dwell therein.

2 For he hath founded it upon the seas; and hath prepared it upon the rivers.

R. **Lord**, this is the people that longs to see your face.

3 Who shall ascend into the mountain of the **Lord**: or who shall stand in his holy place?

4ab The innocent in hands, and clean of heart, who hath not taken his soul in vain.

R. **Lord**, this is the people that longs to see your face.

5 He shall receive a blessing from the **Lord**, and mercy from **God** his Saviour.

6 This is the generation of them that seek him, of them that seek the face of the **God** of Jacob.

R. **Lord**, this is the people that longs to see your face.

Alleluia

R. Alleluia, alleluia.

105 A lamp to my feet is your **word**, a light to my path.

R. Alleluia, alleluia.

Gospel: Mark 4: 21-25

21 And he said to them: Doth a candle come in to be put under a bushel, or under a bed? and not to be set on a candlestick?

22 For there is nothing hid, which shall not be made manifest. neither was it made secret, but that it may come abroad.

23 If any man have ears to hear, let him hear.

24 And he said to them: Take heed what you hear. In what measure you shall mete, it shall be measured to you again, and more shall be given to you.

25 For he that hath, to him shall be given: and he that hath not, that also which he hath shall be taken away from him.

∼

First Reading: Hebrews 10: 32-39

Responsorial Psalm: Psalms 37: 3-4, 5-6, 23-24, 39-40

Alleluia: Matthew 11: 25

Gospel: Mark 4: 26-34

First Reading: Hebrews 10: 32-39

32 But call to mind the former days, wherein, being **illuminated**, you endured a great fight of afflictions.

33 And on the one hand indeed, by reproaches and tribulations, were made a gazingstock; and on the other, became companions of them that were used in such sort.

34 For you both had **compassion** on them that were in bands, and took with joy the being stripped of your own goods, knowing that you have a better and a lasting substance.

35 Do not therefore lose your **confidence**, which hath a great reward.

36 For patience is necessary for you; that, doing the **will** of **God**, you may receive the promise.

37 For yet a little and a very little while, and he that is to come, will come, and will not delay.

38 But my just man liveth by **faith**; but if he withdraw himself, he shall not please my soul.

39 But we are not the children of withdrawing unto perdition, but of **faith** to the saving of the soul.

Responsorial Psalm: Psalms 37: 3-4, 5-6, 23-24, 39-40

R. (39a) The salvation of the just comes from the **Lord**.

3 Trust in the **Lord**, and do good, and dwell in the land, and thou shalt be fed with its riches.

4 Delight in the **Lord**, and he will give thee the requests of thy heart.

R. The salvation of the just comes from the **Lord**.

5 Commit thy way to the **Lord**, and trust in him, and he will do it.

6 And he will bring forth thy justice as the light, and thy judgment as the noonday.

R. The salvation of the just comes from the **Lord**.

23 With the **Lord** shall the steps of a man be directed, and he shall like well his way.

24 When he shall fall he shall not be bruised, for the **Lord** putteth his hand under him.

R. The salvation of the just comes from the **Lord**.

39 But the salvation of the just is from the **Lord**, and he is their protector in the time of trouble.

40 And the **Lord** will help them and deliver them: and he will rescue them from the wicked, and save them, because they have hoped in him.

R. The salvation of the just comes from the **Lord**.

Alleluia

R. Alleluia, alleluia.

25 Blessed are you, **Father**, **Lord** of heaven and earth; you have revealed to little ones the mysteries of the Kingdom.

R. Alleluia, alleluia.

Gospel: Mark 4: 26-34

26 And he said: So is the **kingdom** of **God**, as if a man should cast seed into the earth,

27 And should sleep, and rise, night and day, and the seed should spring, and grow up whilst he knoweth not.

28 For the earth of itself bringeth forth fruit, first the blade, then the ear, afterwards the full corn in the ear.

29 And when the fruit is brought forth, immediately he putteth in the sickle, because the harvest is come.

30 And he said: To what shall we liken the **kingdom** of **God**? or to what parable shall we compare it?

31 It is as a grain of mustard seed: which when it is sown in the earth, is less than all the seeds that are in the earth:

32 And when it is sown, it groweth up, and becometh greater than all herbs, and shooteth out great branches, so that the birds of the air may dwell under the shadow thereof.

33 And with many such parables, he spoke to them the **word**, according as they were able to hear.

34 And without parable he did not speak unto them; but apart, he explained all things to his **disciples**.

REFLECTIONS

REFLECTIONS

Flight into Egypt (1614)
Rubens, Peter Paul Rubens

FEBRUARY 2025

SATURDAY FEBRUARY 1, 2025

First Reading: Hebrews 11: 1-2, 8-19

Responsorial Psalm: Luke 1: 69, 70-72, 73-75

Alleluia: John 3: 16

Gospel: Mark 4: 35-41

First Reading: Hebrews 11: 1-2, 8-19

1 Now faith is the substance of things to be hoped for, the evidence of things that appear not.

2 For by this the ancients obtained a testimony.

8 By faith he that is called Abraham, obeyed to go out into a place which he was to receive for an inheritance; and he went out, not knowing whither he went.

9 By faith he abode in the land, dwelling in cottages, with Isaac and Jacob, the co-heirs of the same promise.

10 For he looked for a city that hath foundations; whose builder and maker is God.

11 By faith also Sara herself, being barren, received strength to conceive seed, even past the time of age; because she believed that he was faithful who had promised,

12 For which cause there sprung even from one (and him as good as dead) as the stars of heaven in multitude, and as the sand which is by the sea shore innumerable.

13 All these died according to faith, not having received the promises, but beholding them afar off, and saluting them, and confessing that they are pilgrims and strangers on the earth.

14 For they that say these things, do signify that they seek a country.

15 And truly if they had been mindful of that from whence they came out, they had doubtless time to return.

16 But now they desire a better, that is to say, a heavenly country. Therefore God is not ashamed to be called their God; for he hath prepared for them a city.

17 By faith Abraham, when he was tried, offered Isaac: and he that had received the promises, offered up his only begotten son;

18 (To whom it was said: In Isaac shall thy seed be called.)

19 Accounting that God is able to raise up even from the dead. Whereupon also he received him for a parable.

Responsorial Psalm: Luke 1: 69, 70-72, 73-75

R. (68) Blessed be the Lord the God of Israel; he has come to his people.

69 And hath raised up an horn of salvation to us, in the house of David his servant:

R. Blessed be the Lord the God of Israel; he has come to his people.

70 As he spoke by the mouth of his holy prophets, who are from the beginning:

71 Salvation from our enemies, and from the hand of all that hate us:

72 To perform mercy to our fathers, and to remember his holy testament,

R. Blessed be the Lord the God of Israel; he has come to his people.

73 The oath, which he swore to Abraham our father, that he would grant to us,

74 That being delivered from the hand of our enemies, we may serve him without fear,

75 In holiness and justice before him, all our days.

R. Blessed be the Lord the God of Israel; he has come to his people.

Alleluia: John 3: 16

R. Alleluia, alleluia.

16 God so loved the world that he gave his only-begotten Son, so that everyone who believes in him might have eternal life.

R. Alleluia, alleluia.

Gospel: Mark 4: 35-41

35 And he saith to them that day, when evening was come: Let us pass over to the other side.

36 And sending away the multitude, they take him even as he was in the ship: and there were other ships with him.

37 And there arose a great storm of wind, and the waves beat into the ship, so that the ship was filled.

38 And he was in the hinder part of the ship, sleeping upon a pillow; and they awake him, and say to him: Master, doth it not concern thee that we perish?

39 And rising up, he rebuked the wind, and said to the sea: Peace, be still. And the wind ceased: and there was made a great calm.

40 And he said to them: Why are you fearful? have you not faith yet?

41 And they feared exceedingly: and they said one to another: Who is this (thinkest thou) that both wind and sea obey him?

~

SUNDAY FEBRUARY 2, 2025

First Reading: Malachi 3: 1-4

Responsorial Psalm: Psalms 24: 7, 8, 9, 10

Second Reading: Hebrews 2: 14-18

Alleluia: Luke 2: 32

Gospel: Luke 2: 22-40 or Luke 2: 22-32

First Reading: Malachi 3: 1-4

1 Behold I send my angel, and he shall prepare the way before my face. And presently the Lord, whom you seek, and the angel of the testament, whom you desire, shall come to his temple. Behold he cometh, saith the Lord of hosts.

2 And who shall be able to think of the day of his coming? and who shall stand to see him? for he is like a refining fire, and like the fuller's herb:

3 And he shall sit refining and cleansing the silver, and he shall purify the sons of Levi, and shall refine them as gold, and as silver, and they shall offer sacrifices to the Lord in justice.

4 And the sacrifice of Juda and of Jerusalem shall please the Lord, as in the days of old, and in the ancient years.

Responsorial Psalm: Psalms 24: 7, 8, 9, 10

R. (8) Who is this king of glory? It is the Lord!

7 Lift up your gates, O ye princes, and be ye lifted up, O eternal gates: and the King of Glory shall enter in.

R. Who is this king of glory? It is the Lord!

8 Who is this King of Glory? the Lord who is strong and mighty: the Lord mighty in battle.

R. Who is this king of glory? It is the Lord!

9 Lift up your gates, O ye princes, and be ye lifted up, O eternal gates: and the King of Glory shall enter in.

R. Who is this king of glory? It is the Lord!

10 Who is this King of Glory? the Lord of hosts, he is the King of Glory.

R. Who is this king of glory? It is the Lord!

Second Reading: Hebrews 2: 14-18

14 Therefore because the children are partakers of flesh and blood, he also himself in like manner hath been partaker of the same: that, through death, he might destroy him who had the empire of death, that is to say, the devil:

15 And might deliver them, who through the fear of death were all their lifetime subject to servitude.

16 For no where doth he take hold of the angels: but of the seed of Abraham he taketh hold.

17 Wherefore it behoved him in all things to be made like unto his brethren, that he might become a merciful and faithful priest before God, that he might be a propitiation for the sins of the people.

18 For in that, wherein he himself hath suffered and been tempted, he is able to succour them also that are tempted.

Alleluia: Luke 2: 32

R. Alleluia, alleluia.

32 A light of revelation to the Gentiles, and glory for your people Israel.

R. Alleluia, alleluia.

Gospel: Luke 2: 22-40 or Luke 2: 22-32

22 And after the days of her purification, according to the law of Moses, were accomplished, they carried him to Jerusalem, to present him to the Lord:

23 As it is written in the law of the Lord: Every male opening the womb shall be called holy to the Lord:

24 And to offer a sacrifice, according as it is written in the law of the Lord, a pair of turtledoves, or two young pigeons:

25 And behold there was a man in Jerusalem named Simeon, and this man was just and devout, waiting for the consolation of Israel; and the Holy Ghost was in him.

26 And he had received an answer from the Holy Ghost, that he should not see death, before he had seen the Christ of the Lord.

27 And he came by the Spirit into the temple. And when his parents brought in the child Jesus, to do for him according to the custom of the law,

28 He also took him into his arms, and blessed God, and said:

29 Now thou dost dismiss thy servant, O Lord, according to thy word in peace;

30 Because my eyes have seen thy salvation,

31 Which thou hast prepared before the face of all peoples:

32 A light to the revelation of the Gentiles, and the glory of thy people Israel.

33 And his father and mother were wondering at those things which were spoken concerning him.

34 And Simeon blessed them, and said to Mary his mother: Behold this child is set for the fall, and for the resurrection of many in Israel, and for a sign which shall be contradicted;

35 And thy own soul a sword shall pierce, that, out of many hearts, thoughts may be revealed.

36 And there was one Anna, a prophetess, the daughter of Phanuel, of the tribe of Aser; she was far advanced in years, and had lived with her husband seven years from her virginity.

37 And she was a widow until fourscore and four years; who departed not from the temple, by fastings and prayers serving night and day.

38 Now she, at the same hour, coming in, confessed to the Lord; and spoke of him to all that looked for the redemption of Israel.

39 And after they had performed all things according to the law of the Lord, they returned into Galilee, to their city Nazareth.

40 And the child grew, and waxed strong, full of wisdom; and the grace of God was in him.

Or

22 And after the days of her purification, according to the law of Moses, were accomplished, they carried him to Jerusalem, to present him to the Lord:

23 As it is written in the law of the Lord: Every male opening the womb shall be called holy to the Lord:

24 And to offer a sacrifice, according as it is written in the law of the Lord, a pair of turtledoves, or two young pigeons:

25 And behold there was a man in Jerusalem named Simeon, and this man was just and devout, waiting for the consolation of Israel; and the Holy Ghost was in him.

26 And he had received an answer from the Holy Ghost, that he should not see death, before he had seen the Christ of the Lord.

27 And he came by the Spirit into the temple. And when his parents brought in the child Jesus, to do for him according to the custom of the law,

28 He also took him into his arms, and blessed God, and said:

29 Now thou dost dismiss thy servant, O Lord, according to thy word in peace;

30 Because my eyes have seen thy salvation,

31 Which thou hast prepared before the face of all peoples:

32 A light to the revelation of the Gentiles, and the glory of thy people Israel.

MONDAY FEBRUARY 3, 2025

First Reading: Hebrews 11: 32-40

Responsorial Psalm: Psalms 31: 20, 21, 22, 23, 24

Alleluia: Luke 7: 16

Gospel: Mark 5: 1-20

First Reading: Hebrews 11:32-40

In this passage, the author reflects on the faith of various biblical figures, such as Gideon, Samson, David, and the prophets. Through their faith, they accomplished great feats, including conquering kingdoms, administering justice, and escaping death. Despite their trials and sufferings, these individuals were steadfast, yet they did not receive the ultimate promise during their lifetimes. This promise is now fulfilled in Christ, who provides something better for us.

Responsorial Psalm: Psalms 31:20-24

The psalmist praises God's protection and mercy, expressing confidence in the Lord's ability to shelter and save those who trust in Him. The response encourages the faithful to take comfort and hope in the Lord, emphasizing His faithfulness to those who love Him and live righteously.

Alleluia: Luke 7:16

This short verse acknowledges the presence of a great prophet in Jesus and the visitation of God among His people, highlighting the significance of Christ's ministry.

Gospel: Mark 5:1-20

This Gospel recounts the dramatic encounter between Jesus and a man possessed by many demons, known as "Legion." Jesus exorcises the demons, sending them into a herd of swine, which then rush into the sea and drown. The man is restored to his right mind, but the locals, fearful of Jesus' power, ask Him to leave their region. The healed man, eager to follow Jesus, is instead instructed to stay and share the story of God's mercy with his community, which he does, causing great wonder among the people.

***

TUESDAY FEBRUARY 4, 2025

Ordinary Weekday

First Reading: Hebrews 12: 1-4

Responsorial Psalm: Psalms 22: 26b-27, 28 and 30, 31-32

Alleluia: Matthew 8: 17

Gospel: Mark 5: 21-43

First Reading: Hebrews 12: 1-4

1 And therefore we also having so great a cloud of witnesses over our head, laying aside every weight and sin which surrounds us, let us run by patience to the fight proposed to us:

2 Looking on Jesus, the author and finisher of faith, who having joy set before him, endured the cross, despising the shame, and now sitteth on the right hand of the throne of God.

3 For think diligently upon him that endured such opposition from sinners against himself; that you be not wearied, fainting in your minds.

4 For you have not yet resisted unto blood, striving against sin:

Responsorial Psalm: Psalms 22: 26b-27, 28 and 30, 31-32

R. (27b) They will praise you, Lord, who long for you.

26b I will pay my vows in the sight of them that fear him.

27 The poor shall eat and shall be filled: and they shall praise the Lord that seek him: their hearts shall live for ever and ever.

R. They will praise you, Lord, who long for you.

28 All the ends of the earth shall remember, and shall be converted to the Lord: And all the kindreds of the Gentiles shall adore in his sight.

30 All the fat ones of the earth have eaten and have adored: all they that go down to the earth shall fall before him.

R. They will praise you, Lord, who long for you.

31 And to him my soul shall live: and my seed shall serve him.

32 There shall be declared to the Lord a generation to come: and the heavens shall shew forth his justice to a people that shall be born, which the Lord hath made.

R. They will praise you, Lord, who long for you.

Alleluia: Matthew 8: 17

R. Alleluia, alleluia.

17 Christ took away our infirmities and bore our diseases.

R. Alleluia, alleluia.

Gospel: Mark 5: 21-43

21 And when Jesus had passed again in the ship over the strait, a great multitude assembled together unto him, and he was nigh unto the sea.

22 And there cometh one of the rulers of the synagogue named Jairus: and seeing him, falleth down at his feet.

23 And he besought him much, saying: My daughter is at the point of death, come, lay thy hand upon her, that she may be safe, and may live.

24 And he went with him, and a great multitude followed him, and they thronged him.

25 And a woman who was under an issue of blood twelve years,

26 And had suffered many things from many physicians; and had spent all that she had, and was nothing the better, but rather worse,

27 When she had heard of Jesus, came in the crowd behind him, and touched his garment.

28 For she said: If I shall touch but his garment, I shall be whole.

29 And forthwith the fountain of her blood was dried up, and she felt in her body that she was healed of the evil.

30 And immediately Jesus knowing in himself the virtue that had proceeded from him, turning to the multitude, said: Who hath touched my garments?

31 And his disciples said to him: Thou seest the multitude thronging thee, and sayest thou who hath touched me?

32 And he looked about to see her who had done this.

33 But the woman fearing and trembling, knowing what was done in her, came and fell down before him, and told him all the truth.

34 And he said to her: Daughter, thy faith hath made thee whole: go in peace, and be thou whole of thy disease.

35 While he was yet speaking, some come from the ruler of the synagogue's house, saying: Thy daughter is dead: why dost thou trouble the master any further?

36 But Jesus having heard the word that was spoken, saith to the ruler of the synagogue: Fear not, only believe.

37 And he admitted not any man to follow him, but Peter, and James, and John the brother of James.

38 And they come to the house of the ruler of the synagogue; and he seeth a tumult, and people weeping and wailing much.

39 And going in, he saith to them: Why make you this ado, and weep? the damsel is not dead, but sleepeth.

40 And they laughed him to scorn. But he having put them all out, taketh the father and the mother of the damsel, and them that were with him, and entereth in where the damsel was lying.

41 And taking the damsel by the hand, he saith to her: Talitha cumi, which is, being interpreted: Damsel (I say to thee) arise.

42 And immediately the damsel rose up, and walked: and she was twelve years old: and they were astonished with a great astonishment.

43 And he charged them strictly that no man should know it: and commanded that something should be given her to eat.

～

WEDNESDAY FEBRUARY 5, 2025

First Reading: Hebrews 12: 4-7, 11-15

Responsorial Psalm: Psalms 103: 1-2, 13-14, 17-18a

Alleluia: John 10: 27

Gospel: Mark 6: 1-6

First Reading: Hebrews 12: 4-7, 11-15

4 For you have not yet resisted unto blood, striving against sin:

5 And you have forgotten the consolation, which speaketh to you, as unto

children, saying: My son, neglect not the discipline of the Lord; neither be thou wearied whilst thou art rebuked by him.

6 For whom the Lord loveth, he chastiseth; and he scourgeth every son whom he receiveth.

7 Persevere under discipline. God dealeth with you as with his sons; for what son is there, whom the father doth not correct?

11 Now all chastisement for the present indeed seemeth not to bring with it joy, but sorrow: but afterwards it will yield, to them that are exercised by it, the most peaceable fruit of justice.

12 Wherefore lift up the hands which hang down, and the feeble knees,

13 And make straight steps with your feet: that no one, halting, may go out of the way; but rather be healed.

14 Follow peace with all men, and holiness: without which no man shall see God.

15 Looking diligently, lest any man be wanting to the grace of God; lest any root of bitterness springing up do hinder, and by it many be defiled.

Responsorial Psalm: Psalms 103: 1-2, 13-14, 17-18a

R. (17) The Lord's kindness is everlasting to those who fear him.

1 Bless the Lord, O my soul: and let all that is within me bless his holy name.

2 Bless the Lord, O my soul, and never forget all he hath done for thee.

R. The Lord's kindness is everlasting to those who fear him.

13 As a father hath compassion on his children, so hath the Lord compassion on them that fear him:

14 For he knoweth our frame. He remembereth that we are dust:

R. The Lord's kindness is everlasting to those who fear him.

17 But the mercy of the Lord is from eternity and unto eternity upon them that fear him: And his justice unto children's children,

18a To such as keep his covenant.

R. The Lord's kindness is everlasting to those who fear him.

Alleluia: John 10: 27

R. Alleluia, alleluia.

27 My sheep hear my voice, says the Lord; I know them, and they follow me.

R. Alleluia, alleluia.

Gospel: Mark 6: 1-6

1 And going out from thence, he went into his own country; and his disciples followed him.

2 And when the sabbath was come, he began to teach in the synagogue: and many hearing him were in admiration at his doctrine, saying: How came this man by all these things? and what wisdom is this that is given to him, and such mighty works as are wrought by his hands?

3 Is not this the carpenter, the son of Mary, the brother of James, and Joseph, and Jude, and Simon? are not also his sisters here with us? And they were scandalized in regard of him.

4 And Jesus said to them: A prophet is not without honor, but in his own country, and in his own house, and among his own kindred.

5 And he could not do any miracles there, only that he cured a few that were sick, laying his hands upon them.

6 And he wondered because of their unbelief, and he went through the villages round about teaching.

∼

THURSDAY FEBRUARY 6, 2025

First Reading: Hebrews 12: 18-19, 21-24

Responsorial Psalm: Psalms 48: 2-3ab, 3cd-4, 9, 10-11

Alleluia: Mark 1: 15

Gospel: Mark 6: 7-13

First Reading: Hebrews 12: 18-19, 21-24

18 For you are not come to a mountain that might be touched, and a burning fire, and a whirlwind, and darkness, and storm,

19 And the sound of a trumpet, and the voice of words, which they that heard excused themselves, that the word might not be spoken to them:

21 And so terrible was that which was seen, Moses said: I am frighted, and tremble.

22 But you are come to mount Sion, and to the city of the living God, the heavenly Jerusalem, and to the company of many thousands of angels,

23 And to the church of the firstborn, who are written in the heavens, and to God the judge of all, and to the spirits of the just made perfect,

24 And to Jesus the mediator of the new testament, and to the sprinkling of blood which speaketh better than that of Abel.

Responsorial Psalm: Psalms 48: 2-3ab, 3cd-4, 9, 10-11

R. (10) O God, we ponder your mercy within your temple.

2 Great is the Lord, and exceedingly to be praised in the city of our God, in his holy mountain.

3ab With the joy of the whole earth.

R. O God, we ponder your mercy within your temple.

3cd Mount Sion founded, on the sides of the north, the city of the great king.

4 In her houses shall God be known, when he shall protect her.

R. O God, we ponder your mercy within your temple.

9 As we have heard, so have we seen, in the city of the Lord of hosts, in the city of our God: God hath founded it for ever.

R. O God, we ponder your mercy within your temple.

10 We have received thy mercy, O God, in the midst of thy temple.

11 According to thy name, O God, so also is thy praise unto the ends of the earth: thy right hand is full of justice.

R. O God, we ponder your mercy within your temple.

Alleluia: Mark 1: 15

R. Alleluia, alleluia.

15 The Kingdom of God is at hand; repent and believe in the Gospel.

R. Alleluia, alleluia.

Gospel: Mark 6: 7-13

7 And he called the twelve; and began to send them two and two, and gave them power over unclean spirits.

8 And he commanded them that they should take nothing for the way, but a staff only: no scrip, no bread, nor money in their purse,

9 But to be shod with sandals, and that they should not put on two coats.

10 And he said to them: Wheresoever you shall enter into an house, there abide till you depart from that place.

11 And whosoever shall not receive you, nor hear you; going forth from thence, shake off the dust from your feet for a testimony to them.

12 And going forth they preached that men should do penance:

13 And they cast out many devils, and anointed with oil many that were sick, and healed them.

～

FRIDAY FEBRUARY 7, 2025

First Reading: Hebrews 13: 1-8

Responsorial Psalm: Psalms 27: 1, 3, 5, 8b-9abc

Alleluia: Luke 8: 15

Gospel: Mark 6: 14-29

First Reading: Hebrews 13: 1-8

1 Let the charity of the brotherhood abide in you.

2 And hospitality do not forget; for by this some, being not aware of it, have entertained angels.

3 Remember them that are in bands, as if you were bound with them; and them that labour, as being yourselves also in the body.

4 Marriage honourable in all, and the bed undefiled. For fornicators and adulterers God will judge.

5 Let your manners be without covetousness, contented with such things as you have; for he hath said: I will not leave thee, neither will I forsake thee.

6 So that we may confidently say: The Lord is my helper: I will not fear what man shall do to me.

7 Remember your prelates who have spoken the word of God to you; whose faith follow, considering the end of their conversation,

8 Jesus Christ, yesterday, and today; and the same for ever.

Responsorial Psalm: Psalms 27: 1, 3, 5, 8b-9abc

R. (1a) The Lord is my light and my salvation.

1 The Lord is my light and my salvation, whom shall I fear? The Lord is the protector of my life: of whom shall I be afraid?

R. The Lord is my light and my salvation.

3 If armies in camp should stand together against me, my heart shall not fear. If a battle should rise up against me, in this will I be confident.

R. The Lord is my light and my salvation.

5 For he hath hidden me in his tabernacle; in the day of evils, he hath protected me in the secret place of his tabernacle.

R. The Lord is my light and my salvation.

8b Thy face, O Lord, will I still seek.

9abc Turn not away thy face from me; decline not in thy wrath from thy servant. Be thou my helper, forsake me not.

R. The Lord is my light and my salvation.

Alleluia: Luke 8: 15

R. Alleluia, alleluia.

15 Blessed are they who have kept the word with a generous heart, and yield a harvest through perseverance.

R. Alleluia, alleluia.

Gospel: Mark 6: 14-29

14 And king Herod heard, (for his name was made manifest,) and he said: John the Baptist is risen again from the dead, and therefore mighty works shew forth themselves in him.

15 And others said: It is Elias. But others said: It is a prophet, as one of the prophets.

16 Which Herod hearing, said: John whom I beheaded, he is risen again from the dead.

17 For Herod himself had sent and apprehended John, and bound him in prison for the sake of Herodias the wife of Philip his brother, because he had married her.

18 For John said to Herod: It is not lawful for thee to have thy brother's wife.

19 Now Herodias laid snares for him: and was desirous to put him to death, and could not.

20 For Herod feared John, knowing him to be a just and holy man: and kept him, and when he heard him, did many things: and he heard him willingly.

21 And when a convenient day was come, Herod made a supper for his birthday, for the princes, and tribunes, and chief men of Galilee.

22 And when the daughter of the same Herodias had come in, and had danced, and pleased Herod, and them that were at table with him, the king said to the damsel: Ask of me what thou wilt, and I will give it thee.

23 And he swore to her: Whatsoever thou shalt ask I will give thee, though it be the half of my kingdom.

24 Who when she was gone out, said to her mother, What shall I ask? But she said: The head of John the Baptist.

25 And when she was come in immediately with haste to the king, she asked, saying: I will that forthwith thou give me in a dish, the head of John the Baptist.

26 And the king was struck sad. Yet because of his oath, and because of them that were with him at table, he would not displease her:

27 But sending an executioner, he commanded that his head should be brought in a dish.

28 And he beheaded him in the prison, and brought his head in a dish: and gave it to the damsel, and the damsel gave it to her mother.

29 Which his disciples hearing came, and took his body, and laid it in a tomb.

～

SATURDAY FEBRUARY 8, 2025

First Reading: Hebrews 13: 15-17, 20-21

Responsorial Psalm: Psalms 23: 1-3a, 3b-4, 5, 6

Alleluia: John 10: 27

Gospel: Mark 6: 30-34

First Reading: Hebrews 13: 15-17, 20-21

15 By him therefore let us offer the sacrifice of praise always to God, that is to say, the fruit of lips confessing to his name.

16 And do not forget to do good, and to impart; for by such sacrifices God's favour is obtained.

17 Obey your prelates, and be subject to them. For they watch as being to render an account of your souls; that they may do this with joy, and not with grief. For this is not expedient for you.

20 And may the God of peace, who brought again from the dead the great pastor of the sheep, our Lord Jesus Christ, in the blood of the everlasting testament,

21 Fit you in all goodness, that you may do his will; doing in you that which is well pleasing in his sight, through Jesus Christ, to whom is glory for ever and ever. Amen.

Responsorial Psalm: Psalms 23: 1-3a, 3b-4, 5, 6

R. (1) The Lord is my shepherd; there is nothing I shall want.

1 The Lord ruleth me: and I shall want nothing.

2 He hath set me in a place of pasture. He hath brought me up, on the water of refreshment:

3a He hath converted my soul.

R. The Lord is my shepherd; there is nothing I shall want.

3b He hath led me on the paths of justice, for his own name's sake.

4 For though I should walk in the midst of the shadow of death, I will fear no evils, for thou art with me. Thy rod and thy staff, they have comforted me.

R. The Lord is my shepherd; there is nothing I shall want.

5 Thou hast prepared a table before me against them that afflict me. Thou hast anointed my head with oil; and my chalice which inebriateth me, how goodly is it!

R. The Lord is my shepherd; there is nothing I shall want.

6 And thy mercy will follow me all the days of my life. And that I may dwell in the house of the Lord unto length of days.

R. The Lord is my shepherd; there is nothing I shall want.

Alleluia: John 10: 27

R. Alleluia, alleluia.

27 My sheep hear my voice, says the Lord; I know them, and they follow me.

R. Alleluia, alleluia.

Gospel: Mark 6: 30-34

30 And the apostles coming together unto Jesus, related to him all things that they had done and taught.

31 And he said to them: Come apart into a desert place, and rest a little. For there were many coming and going: and they had not so much as time to eat.

32 And going up into a ship, they went into a desert place apart.

33 And they saw them going away, and many knew: and they ran flocking thither on foot from all the cities, and were there before them.

34 And Jesus going out saw a great multitude: and he had compassion on them, because they were as sheep not having a shepherd, and he began to teach them many things.

~

SUNDAY FEBRUARY 9, 2025

First Reading: Isaiah 6: 1-2a, 3-8

Responsorial Psalm: Psalms 138: 1-2ab, 2cd-3, 4-5, 7c-8

Second Reading: First Corinthians 15: 1-11 or First Corinthians 15: 3-8, 11

Alleluia: Matthew 4: 19

Gospel: Luke 5: 1-11

First Reading: Isaiah 6: 1-2a, 3-8

1 In the year that king Ozias died, I saw the Lord sitting upon a throne high and elevated: and his train filled the temple.

2a Upon it stood the seraphims.

3 And they cried one to another, and said: Holy, holy, holy, the Lord God of hosts, all the earth is full of his glory.

4 And the lintels of the doors were moved at the voice of him that cried, and the house was filled with smoke.

5 And I said: Woe is me, because I have held my peace; because I am a man of unclean lips, and I dwell in the midst of a people that hath unclean lips, and I have seen with my eyes the King the Lord of hosts.

6 And one of the seraphims flew to me, and in his hand was a live coal, which he had taken with the tongs off the altar.

7 And he touched my mouth, and said: Behold this hath touched thy lips, and thy iniquities shall be taken away, and thy sin shall be cleansed.

8 And I heard the voice of the Lord, saying: Whom shall I send? and who shall go for us? And I said: Lo, here am I, send me.

Responsorial Psalm: Psalms 138: 1-2ab, 2cd-3, 4-5, 7c-8

R. (1c) In the sight of the angels I will sing your praises, Lord.

1 I will praise thee, O lord, with my whole heart: for thou hast heard the words of my mouth. I will sing praise to thee in the sight of his angels:

2ab I will worship towards thy holy temple, and I will give glory to thy name.

R. In the sight of the angels I will sing your praises, Lord.

2cd For thy mercy, and for thy truth: for thou hast magnified thy holy name above all.

3 In what day soever I shall call upon thee, hear me: thou shall multiply strength in my soul.

R. In the sight of the angels I will sing your praises, Lord.

4 May all the kings of the earth give glory to thee: for they have heard all the words of thy mouth.

5 And let them sing in the ways of the Lord: for great is the glory of the Lord.

R. In the sight of the angels I will sing your praises, Lord.

7c Your right hand hath saved me.

8 The Lord will repay for me: thy mercy, O Lord, endureth for ever: O despise not the work of thy hands.

R. In the sight of the angels I will sing your praises, Lord.

Second Reading: First Corinthians 15: 1-11 or First Corinthians 15: 3-8, 11

1 Now I make known unto you, brethren, the gospel which I preached to you, which also you have received, and wherein you stand;

2 By which also you are saved, if you hold fast after what manner I preached unto you, unless you have believed in vain.

3 For I delivered unto you first of all, which I also received: how that Christ died for our sins, according to the scriptures:

4 And that he was buried, and that he rose again the third day, according to the scriptures:

5 And that he was seen by Cephas; and after that by the eleven.

6 Then he was seen by more than five hundred brethren at once: of whom many remain until this present, and some are fallen asleep.

7 After that, he was seen by James, then by all the apostles.

8 And last of all, he was seen also by me, as by one born out of due time.

9 For I am the least of the apostles, who am not worthy to be called an apostle, because I persecuted the church of God.

10 But by the grace of God, I am what I am; and his grace in me hath not been void, but I have laboured more abundantly than all they: yet not I, but the grace of God with me.

11 For whether I, or they, so we preach, and so you have believed.

Or

3 For I delivered unto you first of all, which I also received: how that Christ died for our sins, according to the scriptures:

4 And that he was buried, and that he rose again the third day, according to the scriptures:

5 And that he was seen by Cephas; and after that by the eleven.

6 Then he was seen by more than five hundred brethren at once: of whom many remain until this present, and some are fallen asleep.

7 After that, he was seen by James, then by all the apostles.

8 And last of all, he was seen also by me, as by one born out of due time.

11 For whether I, or they, so we preach, and so you have believed.

Alleluia: Matthew 4: 19

R. Alleluia, alleluia.

19 Come after me and I will make you fishers of men.

R. Alleluia, alleluia.

Gospel: Luke 5: 1-11

1 And it came to pass, that when the multitudes pressed upon him to hear the word of God, he stood by the lake of Genesareth,

2 And saw two ships standing by the lake: but the fishermen were gone out of them, and were washing their nets.

3 And going into one of the ships that was Simon's, he desired him to draw back a little from the land. And sitting he taught the multitudes out of the ship.

4 Now when he had ceased to speak, he said to Simon: Launch out into the deep, and let down your nets for a draught.

5 And Simon answering said to him: Master, we have labored all the night, and have taken nothing: but at thy word I will let down the net.

6 And when they had done this, they enclosed a very great multitude of fishes, and their net broke.

7 And they beckoned to their partners that were in the other ship, that they should come and help them. And they came, and filled both the ships, so that they were almost sinking.

8 Which when Simon Peter saw, he fell down at Jesus' knees, saying: Depart from me, for I am a sinful man, O Lord.

9 For he was wholly astonished, and all that were with him, at the draught of the fishes which they had taken.

10 And so were also James and John the sons of Zebedee, who were Simon's partners. And Jesus saith to Simon: Fear not: from henceforth thou shalt catch men.

11 And having brought their ships to land, leaving all things, they followed him.

∽

MONDAY FEBRUARY 10, 2025

First Reading: Genesis 1: 1-19

Responsorial Psalm: Psalms 104: 1-2a, 5-6, 10 and 12, 24 and 35c

Alleluia: Matthew 4: 23

Gospel: Mark 6: 53-56

First Reading: Genesis 1: 1-19

1 In the beginning, God created heaven and earth.

2 And the earth was void and empty, and darkness was upon the face of the deep; and the spirit of God moved over the waters.

3 And God said: Be light made. And light was made.

4 And God saw the light that it was good; and he divided the light from the darkness.

5 And he called the light Day, and the darkness Night; and there was evening and morning one day.

6 And God said: Let there be a firmament made amidst the waters: and let it divide the waters from the waters.

7 And God made a firmament, and divided the waters that were under the firmament, from those that were above the firmament, and it was so.

8 And God called the firmament, Heaven; and the evening and morning were the second day.

9 God also said: Let the waters that are under the heaven, be gathered together into one place: and let the dry land appear. And it was so done.

10 And God called the dry land, Earth; and the gathering together of the waters, he called Seas. And God saw that it was good.

11 And he said: Let the earth bring forth the green herb, and such as may seed, and the fruit tree yielding fruit after its kind, which may have seed in itself upon the earth. And it was so done.

12 And the earth brought forth the green herb, and such as yieldeth seed according to its kind, and the tree that beareth fruit, having seed each one according to its kind. And God saw that it was good.

13 And the evening and the morning were the third day.

14 And God said: Let there be lights made in the firmament of heaven, to divide the day and the night, and let them be for signs, and for seasons, and for days and years:

15 To shine in the firmament of heaven, and to give light upon the earth. And it was so done.

16 And God made two great lights: a greater light to rule the day; and a lesser light to rule the night: and the stars.

17 And he set them in the firmament of heaven to shine upon the earth.

18 And to rule the day and the night, and to divide the light and the darkness. And God saw that it was good.

19 And the evening and morning were the fourth day.

Responsorial Psalm: Psalms 104: 1-2a, 5-6, 10 and 12, 24 and 35c

R. (31b) May the Lord be glad in his works.

1 For David himself. Bless the Lord, O my soul: O Lord my God, thou art exceedingly great. Thou hast put on praise and beauty:

2a And art clothed with light as with a garment.

R. May the Lord be glad in his works.

5 Who hast founded the earth upon its own bases: it shall not be moved for ever and ever.

6 The deep like a garment is its clothing: above the mountains shall the waters stand.

R. May the Lord be glad in his works.

10 Thou sendest forth springs in the vales: between the midst of the hills the waters shall pass.

12 Over them the birds of the air shall dwell: from the midst of the rocks they shall give forth their voices.

R. May the Lord be glad in his works.

24 How great are thy works, O Lord? thou hast made all things in wisdom: the earth is filled with thy riches.

35c O my soul, bless thou the Lord.

R. May the Lord be glad in his works.

Alleluia: Matthew 4: 23

R. Alleluia, alleluia.

23 Jesus preached the Gospel of the Kingdom and cured every disease among the people.

R. Alleluia, alleluia.

Gospel: Mark 6: 53-56

53 And when they had passed over, they came into the land of Genezareth, and set to the shore.

54 And when they were gone out of the ship, immediately they knew him:

55 And running through that whole country, they began to carry about in beds those that were sick, where they heard he was.

56 And whithersoever he entered, into towns or into villages or cities, they laid the sick in the streets, and besought him that they might touch but the hem of his garment: and as many as touched him were made whole.

~

TUESDAY FEBRUARY 11, 2025

First Reading: Genesis 1: 20 – 2: 4a

Responsorial Psalm: Psalms 8: 4-5, 6-7, 8-9

Alleluia: Psalms 119: 36, 29b

Gospel: Mark 7: 1-13

First Reading: Genesis 1: 20 – 2: 4a

20 God also said: Let the waters bring forth the creeping creature having life, and the fowl that may fly over the earth under the firmament of heaven.

21 And God created the great whales, and every living and moving creature, which the waters brought forth, according to their kinds, and every winged fowl according to its kind. And God saw that it was good.

22 And he blessed them, saying: Increase and multiply, and fill the waters of the sea: and let the birds be multiplied upon the earth.

23 And the evening and morning were the fifth day.

24 And God said: Let the earth bring forth the living creature in its kind, cattle and creeping things, and beasts of the earth, according to their kinds. And it was so done.

25 And God made the beasts of the earth according to their kinds, and cattle, and every thing that creepeth on the earth after its kind. And God saw that it was good.

26 And he said: Let us make man to our image and likeness: and let him have dominion over the fishes of the sea, and the fowls of the air, and the beasts, and the whole earth, and every creeping creature that moveth upon the earth.

27 And God created man to his own image: to the image of God he created him: male and female he created them.

28 And God blessed them, saying: Increase and multiply, and fill the earth, and subdue it, and rule over the fishes of the sea, and the fowls of the air, and all living creatures that move upon the earth.

29 And God said: Behold I have given you every herb bearing seed upon the earth, and all trees that have in themselves seed of their own kind, to be your meat:

30 And to all beasts of the earth, and to every fowl of the air, and to all that move upon the earth, and wherein there is life, that they may have to feed upon. And it was so done.

31 And God saw all the things that he had made, and they were very good. And the evening and morning were the sixth day.

2:1 So the heavens and the earth were finished, and all the furniture of them.

2 And on the seventh day God ended his work which he had made: and he rested on the seventh day from all his work which he had done.

3 And he blessed the seventh day, and sanctified it: because in it he had rested from all his work which God created and made.

4a These are the generations of the heaven and the earth, when they were created.

Responsorial Psalm: Psalms 8: 4-5, 6-7, 8-9

R. (2ab) O Lord, our God, how wonderful your name in all the earth!

4 For I will behold thy heavens, the works of thy fingers: the moon and the stars which thou hast founded.

5 What is man that thou art mindful of him? or the son of man that thou visitest him?

R. O Lord, our God, how wonderful your name in all the earth!

6 Thou hast made him a little less than the angels, thou hast crowned him with glory and honour:

7 And hast set him over the works of thy hands.

R. O Lord, our God, how wonderful your name in all the earth!

8 Thou hast subjected all things under his feet, all sheep and oxen: moreover the beasts also of the fields.

9 The birds of the air, and the fishes of the sea, that pass through the paths of the sea.

R. O Lord, our God, how wonderful your name in all the earth!

Alleluia: Psalms 119: 36, 29b

R. Alleluia, alleluia.

36, 29b Incline my heart, O God, to your decrees; And favor me with your law.

R. Alleluia, alleluia.

Gospel: Mark 7: 1-13

1 And there assembled together unto him the Pharisees and some of the scribes, coming from Jerusalem.

2 And when they had seen some of his disciples eat bread with common, that is, with unwashed hands, they found fault.

3 For the Pharisees, and all the Jews eat not without often washing their hands, holding the tradition of the ancients:

4 And when they come from the market, unless they be washed, they eat not: and many other things there are that have been delivered to them to observe, the washings of cups and of pots, and of brazen vessels, and of beds.

5 And the Pharisees and scribes asked him: Why do not thy disciples walk according to the tradition of the ancients, but they eat bread with common hands?

6 But he answering, said to them: Well did Isaias prophesy of you hypocrites, as it is written: This people honoureth me with their lips, but their heart is far from me.

7 And in vain do they worship me, teaching doctrines and precepts of men.

8 For leaving the commandment of God, you hold the tradition of men, the washing of pots and of cups: and many other things you do like to these.

9 And he said to them: Well do you make void the commandment of God, that you may keep your own tradition.

10 For Moses said: Honour thy father and thy mother; and He that shall curse father or mother, dying let him die.

11 But you say: If a man shall say to his father or mother, Corban, (which is a gift,) whatsoever is from me, shall profit thee.

12 And further you suffer him not to do any thing for his father or mother,

13 Making void the word of God by your own tradition, which you have given forth. And many other such like things you do.

~

WEDNESDAY FEBRUARY 12, 2025

First Reading: Genesis 2: 4b-9, 15-17

Responsorial Psalm: Psalms 104: 1-2a, 27-28, 29bc-30

Alleluia: John 17: 17b, 17a

Gospel: Mark 7: 14-23

First Reading: Genesis 2: 4b-9, 15-17

4b In the day that the Lord God made the heaven and the earth:

5 And every plant of the field before it sprung up in the earth, and every herb of the ground before it grew: for the Lord God had not rained upon the earth; and there was not a man to till the earth.

6 But a spring rose out of the earth, watering all the surface of the earth.

7 And the Lord God formed man of the slime of the earth: and breathed into his face the breath of life, and man became a living soul.

8 And the Lord God had planted a paradise of pleasure from the beginning: wherein he placed man whom he had formed.

9 And the Lord God brought forth of the ground all manner of trees, fair to behold, and pleasant to eat of: the tree of life also in the midst of paradise: and the tree of knowledge of good and evil.

15 And the Lord God took man, and put him into the paradise of pleasure, to dress it, and to keep it.

16 And he commanded him, saying: Of every tree of paradise thou shalt eat:

17 But of the tree of knowledge of good and evil, thou shalt not eat. For in what day soever thou shalt eat of it, thou shalt die the death.

Responsorial Psalm: Psalms 104: 1-2a, 27-28, 29bc-30

R. (1a) O bless the Lord, my soul!

1 Bless the Lord, O my soul: O Lord my God, thou art exceedingly great. Thou hast put on praise and beauty:

2a And art clothed with light as with a garment.

R. O bless the Lord, my soul!

27 All expect of thee that thou give them food in season.

28 What thou givest to them they shall gather up: when thou openest thy hand, they shall all be filled with good.

R. O bless the Lord, my soul!

29bc If thou shalt take away their breath, and they shall fail, and shall return to their dust.

30 Thou shalt send forth thy spirit, and they shall be created: and thou shalt renew the face of the earth.

R. O bless the Lord, my soul!

Alleluia: John 17: 17b, 17a

R. Alleluia, alleluia.

17b, 17a Your word, O Lord, is truth: consecrate us in the truth.

R. Alleluia, alleluia.

Gospel: Mark 7: 14-23

14 And calling again the multitude unto him, he said to them: Hear ye me all, and understand.

15 There is nothing from without a man that entering into him, can defile him. But the things which come from a man, those are they that defile a man.

16 If any man have ears to hear, let him hear.

17 And when he was come into the house from the multitude, his disciples asked him the parable.

18 And he saith to them: So are you also without knowledge? understand you not that every thing from without, entering into a man cannot defile him:

19 Because it entereth not into his heart, but goeth into the belly, and goeth out into the privy, purging all meats?

20 But he said that the things which come out from a man, they defile a man.

21 For from within out of the heart of men proceed evil thoughts, adulteries, fornications, murders,

22 Thefts, covetousness, wickedness, deceit, lasciviousness, an evil eye, blasphemy, pride, foolishness.

23 All these evil things come from within, and defile a man.

⁓

THURSDAY FEBRUARY 13, 2025

First Reading: Genesis 2: 18-25

Responsorial Psalm: Psalms 128: 1-2, 3, 4-5

Alleluia: James 1: 21bc

Gospel: Mark 7: 24-30

First Reading: Genesis 2: 18-25

18 And the Lord God said: It is not good for man to be alone: let us make him a help like unto himself.

19 And the Lord God having formed out of the ground all the beasts of the earth, and all the fowls of the air, brought them to Adam to see what he would call them: for whatsoever Adam called any living creature the same is its name.

20 And Adam called all the beasts by their names, and all the fowls of the air, and all the cattle of the field: but for Adam there was not found a helper like himself.

21 Then the Lord God cast a deep sleep upon Adam: and when he was fast asleep, he took one of his ribs, and filled up flesh for it.

22 And the Lord God built the rib which he took from Adam into a woman: and brought her to Adam.

23 And Adam said: This now is bone of my bones, and flesh of my flesh; she shall be called woman, because she was taken out of man.

24 Wherefore a man shall leave father and mother, and shall cleave to his wife: and they shall be two in one flesh.

25 And they were both naked: to wit, Adam and his wife: and were not ashamed.

Responsorial Psalm: Psalms 128: 1-2, 3, 4-5

R. (1a) Blessed are those who fear the Lord.

1 Blessed are all they that fear the Lord: that walk in his ways.

2 For thou shalt eat the labours of thy hands: blessed art thou, and it shall be well with thee.

R. Blessed are those who fear the Lord.

3 Thy wife as a fruitful vine, on the sides of thy house.

R. Blessed are those who fear the Lord.

4 Behold, thus shall the man be blessed that feareth the Lord.

5 May the Lord bless thee out of Sion: and mayest thou see the good things of Jerusalem all the days of thy life.

R. Blessed are those who fear the Lord.

Alleluia: James 1: 21bc

R. Alleluia, alleluia.

21bc Humbly welcome the word that has been planted in you and is able to save your souls.

R. Alleluia, alleluia.

Gospel: Mark 7: 24-30

24 And rising from thence he went into the coasts of Tyre and Sidon: and entering into a house, he would that no man should know it, and he could not be hid.

25 For a woman as soon as she heard of him, whose daughter had an unclean spirit, came in and fell down at his feet.

26 For the woman was a Gentile, a Syrophenician born. And she besought him that he would cast forth the devil out of her daughter.

27 Who said to her: Suffer first the children to be filled: for it is not good to take the bread of the children, and cast it to the dogs.

28 But she answered and said to him: Yea, Lord; for the whelps also eat under the table of the crumbs of the children.

29 And he said to her: For this saying go thy way, the devil is gone out of thy daughter.

30 And when she was come into her house, she found the girl lying upon the bed, and that the devil was gone out.

~

FRIDAY FEBRUARY 14, 2025

First Reading: Genesis 3: 1-8

Responsorial Psalm: Psalms 32: 1-2, 5, 6, 7

Alleluia: Acts 16: 14b

Gospel: Mark 7: 31-37

First Reading: Genesis 3: 1-8

1 Now the serpent was more subtle than any of the beasts of the earth which the Lord God had made. And he said to the woman: Why hath God commanded you, that you should not eat of every tree of paradise?

2 And the woman answered him, saying: Of the fruit of the trees that are in paradise we do eat:

3 But of the fruit of the tree which is in the midst of paradise, God hath commanded us that we should not eat; and that we should not touch it, lest perhaps we die.

4 And the serpent said to the woman: No, you shall not die the death.

5 For God doth know that in what day soever you shall eat thereof, your eyes shall be opened: and you shall be as Gods, knowing good and evil.

6 And the woman saw that the tree was good to eat, and fair to the eyes, and delightful to behold: and she took of the fruit thereof, and did eat, and gave to her husband who did eat.

7 And the eyes of them both were opened: and when they perceived themselves to be naked, they sewed together fig leaves, and made themselves aprons.

8 And when they heard the voice of the Lord God walking in paradise at the afternoon air, Adam and his wife hid themselves from the face of the Lord God, amidst the trees of paradise.

Responsorial Psalm: Psalms 32: 1-2, 5, 6, 7

R. (1a) Blessed are those whose sins are forgiven.

1 To David himself, understanding. Blessed are they whose iniquities are forgiven, and whose sins are covered.

2 Blessed is the man to whom the Lord hath not imputed sin, and in whose spirit there is no guile.

R. Blessed are those whose sins are forgiven.

5 I have acknowledged my sin to thee, and my injustice I have not concealed. I

said I will confess against myself my injustice to the Lord: and thou hast forgiven the wickedness of my sin.

R. Blessed are those whose sins are forgiven.

6 For this shall every one that is holy pray to thee in a seasonable time. And yet in a flood of many waters, they shall not come nigh unto him.

R. Blessed are those whose sins are forgiven.

7 Thou art my refuge from the trouble which hath encompassed me: my joy, deliver me from them that surround me.

R. Blessed are those whose sins are forgiven.

Alleluia: Acts 16: 14b

R. Alleluia, alleluia.

14b Open our hearts, O Lord, to listen to the words of your Son.

R. Alleluia, alleluia.

Gospel: Mark 7: 31-37

31 And again going out of the coasts of Tyre, he came by Sidon to the sea of Galilee, through the midst of the coasts of Decapolis.

32 And they bring to him one deaf and dumb; and they besought him that he would lay his hand upon him.

33 And taking him from the multitude apart, he put his fingers into his ears, and spitting, he touched his tongue:

34 And looking up to heaven, he groaned, and said to him: Ephpheta, which is, Be thou opened.

35 And immediately his ears were opened, and the string of his tongue was loosed, and he spoke right.

36 And he charged them that they should tell no man. But the more he charged them, so much the more a great deal did they publish it.

37 And so much the more did they wonder, saying: He hath done all things well; he hath made both the deaf to hear, and the dumb to speak.

∾

First Reading: Genesis 3: 9-24

Responsorial Psalm: Psalms 90: 2, 3-4abc, 5-6, 12-13

Alleluia: Matthew 4: 4b

Gospel: Mark 8: 1-10

First Reading: Genesis 3: 9-24

9 And the Lord God called Adam, and said to him: Where art thou?

10 And he said: I heard thy voice in paradise; and I was afraid, because I was naked, and I hid myself.

11 And he said to him: And who hath told thee that thou wast naked, but that thou hast eaten of the tree whereof I commanded thee that thou shouldst not eat?

12 And Adam said: The woman, whom thou gavest me to be my companion, gave me of the tree, and I did eat.

13 And the Lord God said to the woman: Why hast thou done this? And she answered: The serpent deceived me, and I did eat.

14 And the Lord God said to the serpent: Because thou hast done this thing, thou art cursed among all cattle, and beasts of the earth: upon thy breast shalt thou go, and earth shalt thou eat all the days of thy life.

15 I will put enmities between thee and the woman, and thy seed and her seed: she shall crush thy head, and thou shalt lie in wait for her heel.

16 To the woman also he said: I will multiply thy sorrows, and thy conceptions: in sorrow shalt thou bring forth children, and thou shalt be under thy husband's power, and he shall have dominion over thee.

17 And to Adam he said: Because thou hast hearkened to the voice of thy wife, and hast eaten of the tree, whereof I commanded thee that thou shouldst not eat, cursed is the earth in thy work; with labour and toil shalt thou eat thereof all the days of thy life.

18 Thorns and thistles shall it bring forth to thee; and thou shalt eat the herbs of the earth.

19 In the sweat of thy face shalt thou eat bread till thou return to the earth, out of which thou wast taken: for dust thou art, and into dust thou shalt return.

20 And Adam called the name of his wife Eve: because she was the mother of all the living.

21 And the Lord God made for Adam and his wife, garments of skins, and clothed them.

22 And he said: Behold Adam is become as one of us, knowing good and evil: now, therefore, lest perhaps he put forth his hand, and take also of the tree of life, and eat, and live for ever.

23 And the Lord God sent him out of the paradise of pleasure, to till the earth from which he was taken.

24 And he cast out Adam; and placed before the paradise of pleasure Cherubims, and a flaming sword, turning every way, to keep the way of the tree of life.

Responsorial Psalm: Psalms 90: 2, 3-4abc, 5-6, 12-13

R. (1) In every age, O Lord, you have been our refuge.

2 Before the mountains were made, or the earth and the world was formed; from eternity and to eternity thou art God.

R. In every age, O Lord, you have been our refuge.

3 Turn not man away to be brought low: and thou hast said: Be converted, O ye sons of men.

4abc For a thousand years in thy sight are as yesterday, which is past. And as a watch in the night.

R. In every age, O Lord, you have been our refuge.

5 Things that are counted nothing, shall their years be.

6 In the morning man shall grow up like grass; in the morning he shall flourish and pass away: in the evening he shall fall, grow dry, and wither.

R. In every age, O Lord, you have been our refuge.

12 Can number thy wrath? So make thy right hand known: and men learned in heart, in wisdom.

13 Return, O Lord, how long? and be entreated in favour of thy servants.

R. In every age, O Lord, you have been our refuge.

Alleluia: Matthew 4: 4b

R. Alleluia, alleluia.

4b One does not live on bread alone, but on every word that comes forth from the mouth of God.

R. Alleluia, alleluia.

Gospel: Mark 8: 1-10

1 In those days again, when there was a great multitude, and had nothing to eat; calling his disciples together, he saith to them:

2 I have compassion on the multitude, for behold they have now been with me three days, and have nothing to eat.

3 And if I shall send them away fasting to their home, they will faint in the way; for some of them came from afar off.

4 And his disciples answered him: From whence can any one fill them here with bread in the wilderness?

5 And he asked them: How many loaves have ye? Who said: Seven.

6 And taking the seven loaves, giving thanks, he broke, and gave to his disciples for to set before them; and they set them before the people.

7 And they had a few little fishes; and he blessed them, and commanded them to be set before them.

8 And they did eat and were filled; and they took up that which was left of the fragments, seven baskets.

9 And they that had eaten were about four thousand; and he sent them away.

10 And immediately going up into a ship with his disciples, he came into the parts of Dalmanutha.

~

First Reading: Jeremiah 17: 5-8

Responsorial Psalm: Psalms 1: 1-2, 3, 4 and 6

Second Reading: First Corinthians 15: 12, 16-20

Alleluia: Luke 6: 23ab

Gospel: Luke 6: 17, 20-26

First Reading: Jeremiah 17: 5-8

5 Thus saith the Lord: Cursed be the man that trusteth in man, and maketh flesh his arm, and whose heart departeth from the Lord.

6 For he shall be like tamaric in the desert, and he shall not see when good shall come: but he shall dwell in dryness in the desert in a salt land, and not inhabited.

7 Blessed be the man that trusteth in the Lord, and the Lord shall be his confidence.

8 And he shall be as a tree that is planted by the waters, that spreadeth out its roots towards moisture: and it shall not fear when the heat cometh. And the leaf thereof shall be green, and in the time of drought it shall not be solicitous, neither shall it cease at any time to bring forth fruit.

Responsorial Psalm: Psalms 1: 1-2, 3, 4 and 6

R. (40:5a) Blessed are they who hope in the Lord.

1 Blessed is the man who hath not walked in the counsel of the ungodly, nor stood in the way of sinners, nor sat in the chair of pestilence.

2 But his will is in the law of the Lord, and on his law he shall meditate day and night.

R. Blessed are they who hope in the Lord.

3 And he shall be like a tree which is planted near the running waters, which shall bring forth its fruit, in due season. And his leaf shall not fall off: and all whatsoever he shall do shall prosper.

214

R. Blessed are they who hope in the Lord.

4 Not so the wicked, not so: but like the dust, which the wind driveth from the face of the earth.

6 For the Lord knoweth the way of the just: and the way of the wicked shall perish.

R. Blessed are they who hope in the Lord.

Second Reading: First Corinthians 15: 12, 16-20

12 Now if Christ be preached, that he arose again from the dead, how do some among you say, that there is no resurrection of the dead?

16 For if the dead rise not again, neither is Christ risen again.

17 And if Christ be not risen again, your faith is vain, for you are yet in your sins.

18 Then they also that are fallen asleep in Christ, are perished.

19 If in this life only we have hope in Christ, we are of all men most miserable.

20 But now Christ is risen from the dead, the first fruits of them that sleep:

Alleluia: Luke 6: 23ab

R. Alleluia, alleluia.

23ab Rejoice and be glad; your reward will be great in heaven.

R. Alleluia, alleluia.

Gospel: Luke 6: 17, 20-26

17 And coming down with them, he stood in a plain place, and the company of his disciples, and a very great multitude of people from all Judea and Jerusalem, and the sea coast both of Tyre and Sidon,

20 And he, lifting up his eyes on his disciples, said: Blessed are ye poor, for yours is the kingdom of God.

21 Blessed are ye that hunger now: for you shall be filled. Blessed are ye that weep now: for you shall laugh.

22 Blessed shall you be when men shall hate you, and when they shall separate

you, and shall reproach you, and cast out your name as evil, for the Son of man's sake.

23 Be glad in that day and rejoice; for behold, your reward is great in heaven. For according to these things did their fathers to the prophets.

24 But woe to you that are rich: for you have your consolation.

25 Woe to you that are filled: for you shall hunger. Woe to you that now laugh: for you shall mourn and weep.

26 Woe to you when men shall bless you: for according to these things did their fathers to the false prophets.

~

MONDAY FEBRUARY 17, 2025

First Reading: Genesis 4: 1-15, 25

Responsorial Psalm: Psalms 50: 1 and 8, 16bc-17, 20-21

Alleluia: John 14: 6

Gospel: Mark 8: 11-13

First Reading: Genesis 4: 1-15, 25

1 And Adam knew Eve his wife: who conceived and brought forth Cain, saying: I have gotten a man through God.

2 And again she brought forth his brother Abel. And Abel was a shepherd, and Cain a husbandman.

3 And it came to pass after many days, that Cain offered, of the fruits of the earth, gifts to the Lord.

4 Abel also offered of the firstlings of his flock, and of their fat: and the Lord had respect to Abel, and to his offerings.

5 But to Cain and his offerings he had no respect: and Cain was exceedingly angry, and his countenance fell.

6 And the Lord said to him: Why art thou angry? and why is thy countenance fallen?

7 If thou do well, shalt thou not receive? but if ill, shall not sin forthwith be present at the door? but the lust thereof shall be under thee, and thou shalt have dominion over it.

8 And Cain said to Abel his brother: Let us go forth abroad. And when they were in the field, Cain rose up against his brother Abel, and slew him.

9 And the Lord said to Cain: Where is thy brother Abel? And he answered, I know not: am I my brother's keeper?

10 And he said to him: What hast thou done? the voice of thy brother's blood crieth to me from the earth.

11 Now, therefore, cursed shalt thou be upon the earth, which hath opened her mouth and received the blood of thy brother at thy hand.

12 When thou shalt till it, it shall not yield to thee its fruit: a fugitive and a vagabond shalt thou be upon the earth.

13 And Cain said to the Lord: My iniquity is greater than that I may deserve pardon.

14 Behold thou dost cast me out this day from the face of the earth, and I shall be hidden from thy face, and I shall be a vagabond and a fugitive on the earth: every one, therefore, that findeth me, shall kill me.

15 And the Lord said to him: No, it shall not be so: but whosoever shall kill Cain, shall be punished sevenfold. And the Lord set a mark upon Cain, that whosoever found him should not kill him.

25 Adam also knew his wife again: and she brought forth a son, and called his name Seth, saying: God hath given me another seed, for Abel whom Cain slew.

Responsorial Psalm: Psalms 50: 1 and 8, 16bc-17, 20-21

R. (14a) Offer to God a sacrifice of praise.

1 The God of gods, the Lord hath spoken: and he hath called the earth. From the rising of the sun, to the going down thereof:

8 I will not reprove thee for thy sacrifices: and thy burnt offerings are always in my sight.

R. Offer to God a sacrifice of praise.

16bc Why dost thou declare my justices, and take my covenant in thy mouth?

17 Seeing thou hast hated discipline: and hast cast my words behind thee.

R. Offer to God a sacrifice of praise.

20 Sitting thou didst speak against thy brother, and didst lay a scandal against thy mother's son:

21 These things hast thou done, and I was silent. Thou thoughtest unjustly that I should be like to thee: but I will reprove thee, and set before thy face.

R. Offer to God a sacrifice of praise.

Alleluia: John 14: 6

R. Alleluia, alleluia.

6 I am the way and the truth and the life, says the Lord; no one comes to the Father except through me.

R. Alleluia, alleluia.

Gospel: Mark 8: 11-13

11 And the Pharisees came forth, and began to question with him, asking him a sign from heaven, tempting him.

12 And sighing deeply in spirit, he saith: Why doth this generation seek a sign? Amen, I say to you, a sign shall not be given to this generation.

13 And leaving them, he went up again into the ship, and passed to the other side of the water.

~

TUESDAY FEBRUARY 18, 2025

First Reading: Genesis 6: 5-8; 7: 1-5, 10

Responsorial Psalm: Psalms 29: 1a and 2, 3ac-4, 3b and 9c-10

Alleluia: John 14: 23

Gospel: Mark 8: 14-21

First Reading: Genesis 6: 5-8; 7: 1-5, 10

5 And God seeing that the wickedness of men was great on the earth, and that all the thought of their heart was bent upon evil at all times,

6 It repented him that he had made man on the earth. And being touched inwardly with sorrow of heart,

7 He said: I will destroy man, whom I have created, from the face of the earth, from man even to beasts, from the creeping thing even to the fowls of the air, for it repenteth me that I have made them.

8 But Noe found grace before the Lord.

7:1 And the Lord said to him: Go in thou and all thy house into the ark: for thee I have seen just before me in this generation.

2 Of all clean beasts take seven and seven, the male and the female.

3 But of the beasts that are unclean two and two, the male and the female. Of the fowls also of the air seven and seven, the male and the female: that seed may be saved upon the face of the whole earth.

4 For yet a while, and after seven days, I will rain upon the earth forty days and forty nights; and I will destroy every substance that I have made, from the face of the earth.

5 And Noe did all things which the Lord had commanded him.

10 And after the seven days were passed, the waters of the flood overflowed the earth.

Responsorial Psalm: Psalms 29: 1a and 2, 3ac-4, 3b and 9c-10

R. (11b) The Lord will bless his people with peace.

1a Bring to the Lord, O ye children of God.

2 Bring to the Lord glory and honour: bring to the Lord glory to his name: adore ye the Lord in his holy court.

R. The Lord will bless his people with peace.

3ac The voice of the Lord is upon the waters; The Lord is upon many waters.

4 The voice of the Lord is in power; the voice of the Lord in magnificence.

R. The Lord will bless his people with peace.

3b The God of majesty hath thundered.

9c The voice of the Lord prepareth the stags: and he will discover the thick woods: and in his temple all shall speak his glory.

10 The Lord maketh the flood to dwell: and the Lord shall sit king for ever.

R. The Lord will bless his people with peace.

Alleluia: John 14: 23

R. Alleluia, alleluia.

23 Whoever loves me will keep my word, says the Lord; and my Father will love him and we will come to him.

R. Alleluia, alleluia.

Gospel: Mark 8: 14-21

14 And they forgot to take bread; and they had but one loaf with them in the ship.

15 And he charged them, saying: Take heed and beware of the leaven of the Pharisees, and of the leaven of Herod.

16 And they reasoned among themselves, saying: Because we have no bread.

17 Which Jesus knowing, saith to them: Why do you reason, because you have no bread? do you not yet know nor understand? have you still your heart blinded?

18 Having eyes, see you not? and having ears, hear you not? neither do you remember.

19 When I broke the five loaves among five thousand, how many baskets full of fragments took you up? They say to him, Twelve.

20 When also the seven loaves among four thousand, how many baskets of fragments took you up? And they say to him, Seven.

21 And he said to them: How do you not yet understand?

First Reading: Genesis 8: 6-13, 20-22

Responsorial Psalm: Psalms 116: 12-13, 14-15, 18-19

Alleluia: Ephesians 1: 17-18

Gospel: Mark 8: 22-26

First Reading: Genesis 8: 6-13, 20-22

6 And after that forty days were passed, Noe, opening the window of the ark which he had made, sent forth a raven:

7 Which went forth and did not return, till the waters were dried up upon the earth.

8 He sent forth also a dove after him, to see if the waters had now ceased upon the face of the earth.

9 But she, not finding where her foot might rest, returned to him into the ark: for the waters were upon the whole earth: and he put forth his hand, and caught her, and brought her into the ark.

10 And having waited yet seven other days, he again sent forth the dove out of the ark.

11 And she came to him in the evening, carrying a bough of an olive tree, with green leaves, in her mouth. Noe therefore understood that the waters were ceased upon the earth.

12 And he stayed yet other seven days: and he sent forth the dove, which returned not any more unto him.

13 Therefore in the six hundredth and first year, the first month, the first day of the month, the waters were lessened upon the earth, and Noe opening the covering of the ark, looked, and saw that the face of the earth was dried.

20 And Noe built an altar unto the Lord: and taking of all cattle and fowls that were clean, offered holocausts upon the altar.

21 And the Lord smelled a sweet savour, and said: I will no more curse the earth for the sake of man: for the imagination and thought of man's heart are

prone to evil from his youth: therefore I will no more destroy every living soul as I have done.

22 All the days of the earth, seedtime and harvest, cold and heat, summer and winter, night and day, shall not cease.

Responsorial Psalm: Psalms 116: 12-13, 14-15, 18-19

R. (17a) To you, Lord, I will offer a sacrifice of praise.

or

R. Alleluia.

12 What shall I render to the Lord, for all the things he hath rendered unto me?

13 I will take the chalice of salvation; and I will call upon the name of the Lord.

R. To you, Lord, I will offer a sacrifice of praise.

or

R. Alleluia.

14 I will pay my vows to the Lord before all his people:

15 Precious in the sight of the Lord is the death of his saints.

R. To you, Lord, I will offer a sacrifice of praise.

or

R. Alleluia.

18 I will pay my vows to the Lord in the sight of all his people:

19 In the courts of the house of the Lord, in the midst of thee, O Jerusalem.

R. To you, Lord, I will offer a sacrifice of praise.

or

R. Alleluia.

Alleluia: Ephesians 1: 17-18

R. Alleluia, alleluia.

17-18 May the Father of our Lord Jesus Christ enlighten the eyes of our hearts, that we may know what is the hope that belongs to his call.

R. Alleluia, alleluia.

Gospel: Mark 8: 22-26

22 And they came to Bethsaida; and they bring to him a blind man, and they besought him that he would touch him.

23 And taking the blind man by the hand, he led him out of the town; and spitting upon his eyes, laying his hands on him, he asked him if he saw any thing.

24 And looking up, he said: I see men as it were trees, walking.

25 After that again he laid his hands upon his eyes, and he began to see, and was restored, so that he saw all things clearly.

26 And he sent him into his house, saying: Go into thy house, and if thou enter into the town, tell nobody.

∼

THURSDAY FEBRUARY 20, 2025

First Reading: Genesis 9: 1-13

Responsorial Psalm: Psalms 102: 16-18, 19-21, 29 and 22-23

Alleluia: John 6: 63c, 68c

Gospel: Mark 8: 27-33

First Reading: Genesis 9: 1-13

1 And God blessed Noe and his sons. And he said to them: Increase and multiply, and fill the earth.

2 And let the fear and dread of you be upon all the beasts of the earth, and upon all the fowls of the air, and all that move upon the earth: all the fishes of the sea are delivered into your hand.

3 And every thing that moveth and liveth shall be meat for you: even as the green herbs have I delivered them all to you:

4 Saving that flesh with blood you shall not eat.

5 For I will require the blood of your lives at the hand of every beast, and at the hand of man, at the hand of every man, and of his brother, will I require the life of man.

6 Whosoever shall shed man's blood, his blood shall be shed: for man was made to the image of God.

7 But increase you and multiply, and go upon the earth, and fill it.

8 Thus also said God to Noe, and to his sons with him,

9 Behold I will establish my covenant with you, and with your seed after you:

10 And with every living soul that is with you, as well in all birds as in cattle and beasts of the earth, that are come forth out of the ark, and in all the beasts of the earth.

11 I will establish my covenant with you, and all flesh shall be no more destroyed with the waters of a flood, neither shall there be from henceforth a flood to waste the earth.

12 And God said: This is the sign of the covenant which I give between me and you, and to every living soul that is with you, for perpetual generations.

13 I will set my bow in the clouds, and it shall be the sign of a covenant between me, and between the earth.

Responsorial Psalm: Psalms 102: 16-18, 19-21, 29 and 22-23

R. (20b) From heaven the Lord looks down on the earth.

16 And the Gentiles shall fear thy name, O Lord, and all the kings of the earth thy glory.

17 For the Lord hath built up Sion: and he shall be seen in his glory.

18 He hath had regard to the prayer of the humble: and he hath not despised their petition.

R. From heaven the Lord looks down on the earth.

19 Let these things be written unto another generation: and the people that shall be created shall praise the Lord:

20 Because he hath looked forth from his high sanctuary: from heaven the Lord hath looked upon the earth.

21 That he might hear the groans of them that are in fetters: that he might release the children of the slain.

R. From heaven the Lord looks down on the earth.

29 The children of thy servants shall continue: and their seed shall be directed for ever.

22 That they may declare the name of the Lord in Sion: and his praise in Jerusalem;

23 When the people assemble together, and kings, to serve the Lord.

R. From heaven the Lord looks down on the earth.

Alleluia: John 6: 63c, 68c

R. Alleluia, alleluia.

63c, 68c Your words, Lord, are Spirit and life; you have the words of everlasting life.

R. Alleluia, alleluia.

Gospel: Mark 8: 27-33

27 And Jesus went out, and his disciples, into the towns of Caesarea Philippi. And in the way, he asked his disciples, saying to them: Whom do men say that I am?

28 Who answered him, saying: John the Baptist; but some Elias, and others as one of the prophets.

29 Then he saith to them: But whom do you say that I am? Peter answering said to him: Thou art the Christ.

30 And he strictly charged them that they should not tell any man of him.

31 And he began to teach them, that the Son of man must suffer many things, and be rejected by the ancients and by the high priests, and the scribes, and be killed: and after three days rise again.

32 And he spoke the word openly. And Peter taking him, began to rebuke him.

33 Who turning about and seeing his disciples, threatened Peter, saying: Go behind me, Satan, because thou savorest not the things that are of God, but that are of men.

∾

FRIDAY FEBRUARY 21, 2025

First Reading: Genesis 11: 1-9

Responsorial Psalm: Psalms 33: 10-11, 12-13, 14-15

Alleluia: John 15: 15b

Gospel: Mark 8: 34 – 9:1

First Reading: Genesis 11: 1-9

1 And the earth was of one tongue, and of the same speech.

2 And when they removed from the east, they found a plain in the land of Sennaar, and dwelt in it.

3 And each one said to his neighbour: Come, let us make brick, and bake them with fire. And they had brick instead of stones, and slime instead of mortar.

4 And they said: Come, let us make a city and a tower, the top whereof may reach to heaven: and let us make our name famous before we be scattered abroad into all lands.

5 And the Lord came down to see the city and the tower, which the children of Adam were building.

6 And he said: Behold, it is one people, and all have one tongue: and they have begun to do this, neither will they leave off from their designs, till they accomplish them in deed.

7 Come ye, therefore, let us go down, and there confound their tongue, that they may not understand one another's speech.

8 And so the Lord scattered them from that place into all lands, and they ceased to build the city.

9 And therefore the name thereof was called Babel, because there the language of the whole earth was confounded: and from thence the Lord scattered them abroad upon the face of all countries.

Responsorial Psalm: Psalms 33: 10-11, 12-13, 14-15

R. (12) Blessed the people the Lord has chosen to be his own.

10 The Lord bringeth to naught the counsels of nations; and he rejecteth the devices of people, and casteth away the counsels of princes.

11 But the counsel of the Lord standeth for ever: the thoughts of his heart to all generations.

R. Blessed the people the Lord has chosen to be his own.

12 Blessed is the nation whose God is the Lord: the people whom he hath chosen for his inheritance.

13 The Lord hath looked from heaven: he hath beheld all the sons of men.

R. Blessed the people the Lord has chosen to be his own.

14 From his habitation which he hath prepared, he hath looked upon all that dwell on the earth.

15 He who hath made the hearts of every one of them: who understandeth all their works.

R. Blessed the people the Lord has chosen to be his own.

Alleluia: John 15: 15b

R. Alleluia, alleluia.

15b I call you my friends, says the Lord, for I have made known to you all that the Father has told me.

R. Alleluia, alleluia.

Gospel: Mark 8: 34 – 9:1

34 And calling the multitude together with his disciples, he said to them: If any man will follow me, let him deny himself, and take up his cross, and follow me.

35 For whosoever will save his life, shall lose it: and whosoever shall lose his life for my sake and the gospel, shall save it.

36 For what shall it profit a man, if he gain the whole world, and suffer the loss of his soul?

37 Or what shall a man give in exchange for his soul?

38 For he that shall be ashamed of me, and of my words, in this adulterous and sinful generation: the Son of man also will be ashamed of him, when he shall come in the glory of his Father with the holy angels.

9:1 And he said to them: Amen I say to you, that there are some of them that stand here, who shall not taste death, till they see the kingdom of God coming in power.

～

SATURDAY FEBRUARY 22, 2025

First Reading: First Peter 5: 1-4

Responsorial Psalm: Psalms 23: 1-3a, 4, 5, 6

Alleluia: Matthew 16: 18

Gospel: Matthew 16: 13-19

First Reading: First Peter 5: 1-4

1 The ancients therefore that are among you, I beseech, who am myself also an ancient, and a witness of the sufferings of Christ: as also a partaker of that glory which is to be revealed in time to come:

2 Feed the flock of God which is among you, taking care of it, not by constraint, but willingly, according to God: not for filthy lucre's sake, but voluntarily:

3 Neither as lording it over the clergy, but being made a pattern of the flock from the heart.

4 And when the prince of pastors shall appear, you shall receive a never fading crown of glory.

Responsorial Psalm: Psalms 23: 1-3a, 4, 5, 6

R. (1) The Lord is my shepherd; there is nothing I shall want.

1 The Lord ruleth me: and I shall want nothing.

2 He hath set me in a place of pasture. He hath brought me up, on the water of refreshment:

3a He hath converted my soul.

R. The Lord is my shepherd; there is nothing I shall want.

4 For though I should walk in the midst of the shadow of death, I will fear no evils, for thou art with me. Thy rod and thy staff, they have comforted me.

R. The Lord is my shepherd; there is nothing I shall want.

5 Thou hast prepared a table before me against them that afflict me. Thou hast anointed my head with oil; and my chalice which inebriateth me, how goodly is it!

R. The Lord is my shepherd; there is nothing I shall want.

6 And thy mercy will follow me all the days of my life. And that I may dwell in the house of the Lord unto length of days.

R. The Lord is my shepherd; there is nothing I shall want.

Alleluia: Matthew 16: 18

R. Alleluia, alleluia.

18 You are Peter, and upon this rock I will build my Church; the gates of the netherworld shall not prevail against it.

R. Alleluia, alleluia.

Gospel: Matthew 16: 13-19

13 And Jesus came into the quarters of Caesarea Philippi: and he asked his disciples, saying: Whom do men say that the Son of man is?

14 But they said: Some John the Baptist, and other some Elias, and others Jeremias, or one of the prophets.

15 Jesus saith to them: But whom do you say that I am?

16 Simon Peter answered and said: Thou art Christ, the Son of the living God.

17 And Jesus answering, said to him: Blessed art thou, Simon Bar-Jona:

because flesh and blood hath not revealed it to thee, but my Father who is in heaven.

18 And I say to thee: That thou art Peter; and upon this rock I will build my church, and the gates of hell shall not prevail against it.

19 And I will give to thee the keys of the kingdom of heaven. And whatsoever thou shalt bind upon earth, it shall be bound also in heaven: and whatsoever thou shalt loose upon earth, it shall be loosed also in heaven.

~

SUNDAY FEBRUARY 23, 2025

First Reading: First Samuel 26: 2, 7-9, 12-13, 22-23

Responsorial Psalm: Psalms 103: 1-2, 3-4, 8, 10, 12-13

Second Reading: First Corinthians 15: 45-49

Alleluia: John 13: 34

Gospel: Luke 6: 27-38

First Reading: First Samuel 26: 2, 7-9, 12-13, 22-23

2 Saul arose, and went down to the wilderness of Ziph, having with him three thousand chosen men of Israel, to seek David in the wilderness of Ziph.

7 So David and Abisai came to the people by night, and found Saul lying and sleeping in the tent, and his spear fixed in the ground at his head: and Abner and the people sleeping round about him.

8 And Abisai said to David: God hath shut up thy enemy this day into thy hands: now then I will run him through with my spear even to the earth at once, and there shall be no need of a second time.

9 And David said to Abisai: Kill him not: for who shall put forth his hand against the Lord's anointed, and shall be guiltless?

12 So David took the spear, and the cup of water which was at Saul's head,

and they went away: and no man saw it, or knew it, or awaked, but they were all asleep, for a deep sleep from the Lord was fallen upon them.

13 And when David was gone over to the other side. and stood on the top of the hill afar off, and a good space was between them,

22 And David answering, said: Behold the king's spear: let one of the king's servants come over and fetch it.

23 And the Lord will reward every one according to his justice, and his faithfulness: for the Lord hath delivered thee this day into my hand, and I would not put forth my hand against the Lord's anointed.

Responsorial Psalm: Psalms 103: 1-2, 3-4, 8, 10, 12-13

R. (8a) The Lord is kind and merciful.

1 Bless the Lord, O my soul: and let all that is within me bless his holy name.

2 Bless the Lord, O my soul, and never forget all he hath done for thee.

R. The Lord is kind and merciful.

3 Who forgiveth all thy iniquities: who healeth all thy diseases.

4 Who redeemeth thy life from destruction: who crowneth thee with mercy and compassion.

R. The Lord is kind and merciful.

8 The Lord is compassionate and merciful: longsuffering and plenteous in mercy.

10 He hath not dealt with us according to our sins: nor rewarded us according to our iniquities.

R. The Lord is kind and merciful.

12 As far as the east is from the west, so far hath he removed our iniquities from us.

13 As a father hath compassion on his children, so hath the Lord compassion on them that fear him:

R. The Lord is kind and merciful.

Second Reading: First Corinthians 15: 45-49

45 The first man Adam was made into a living soul; the last Adam into a quickening spirit.

46 Yet that was not first which is spiritual, but that which is natural; afterwards that which is spiritual.

47 The first man was of the earth, earthly: the second man, from heaven, heavenly.

48 Such as is the earthly, such also are the earthly: and such as is the heavenly, such also are they that are heavenly.

49 Therefore as we have borne the image of the earthly, let us bear also the image of the heavenly.

Alleluia: John 13: 34

R. Alleluia, alleluia.

34 I give you a new commandment, says the Lord: love one another as I have loved you.

R. Alleluia, alleluia.

Gospel: Luke 6: 27-38

27 But I say to you that hear: Love your enemies, do good to them that hate you.

28 Bless them that curse you, and pray for them that calumniate you.

29 And to him that striketh thee on the one cheek, offer also the other. And him that taketh away from thee thy cloak, forbid not to take thy coat also.

30 Give to every one that asketh thee, and of him that taketh away thy goods, ask them not again.

31 And as you would that men should do to you, do you also to them in like manner.

32 And if you love them that love you, what thanks are to you? for sinners also love those that love them.

33 And if you do good to them who do good to you, what thanks are to you? for sinners also do this.

34 And if you lend to them of whom you hope to receive, what thanks are to you? for sinners also lend to sinners, for to receive as much.

35 But love ye your enemies: do good, and lend, hoping for nothing thereby: and your reward shall be great, and you shall be the sons of the Highest; for he is kind to the unthankful, and to the evil.

36 Be ye therefore merciful, as your Father also is merciful.

37 Judge not, and you shall not be judged. Condemn not, and you shall not be condemned. Forgive, and you shall be forgiven.

38 Give, and it shall be given to you: good measure and pressed down and shaken together and running over shall they give into your bosom. For with the same measure that you shall mete withal, it shall be measured to you again.

∼

MONDAY FEBRUARY 24, 2025

First Reading: Sirach 1: 1-10

Responsorial Psalm: Psalms 93: 1ab, 1cd-2, 5

Alleluia: Second Timothy 1: 10

Gospel: Mark 9: 14-29

First Reading: Sirach 1: 1-10

1 All wisdom is from the Lord God, and hath been always with him, and is before all time.

2 Who hath numbered the sand of the sea, and the drops of rain, and the days of the world? Who hath measured the height of heaven, and the breadth of the earth, and the depth of the abyss?

3 Who hath searched out the wisdom of God that goeth before all things?

4 Wisdom hath been created before all things, and the understanding of prudence from everlasting. The word of God on high is the fountain of wisdom, and her ways are everlasting commandments.

233

5 To whom hath the root of wisdom been revealed, and who hath known her wise counsels? To whom hath the discipline of wisdom been revealed and made manifest? and who hath understood the multiplicity of her steps?

6 There is one most high Creator Almighty, and a powerful king, and greatly to be feared, who sitteth upon his throne, and is the God of dominion.

7 He created her in the Holy Ghost, and saw her, and numbered her, and measured her.

8 And he poured her out upon all his works, and upon all flesh according to his gift, and hath given her to them that love him.

9 The fear of the Lord is honour, and glory, and gladness, and a crown of joy.

10 The fear of the Lord shall delight the heart, and shall give joy, and gladness, and length of days.

Responsorial Psalm: Psalms 93: 1ab, 1cd-2, 5

R. (1a) The Lord is king; he is robed in majesty.

1ab The Lord hath reigned, he is clothed with beauty: the Lord is clothed with strength.

R. The Lord is king; he is robed in majesty.

1cd And hath girded himself. For he hath established the world which shall not be moved.

2 Thy throne is prepared from of old: thou art from everlasting.

R. The Lord is king; he is robed in majesty.

5 Thy testimonies are become exceedingly credible: holiness becometh thy house, O Lord, unto length of days.

R. The Lord is king; he is robed in majesty.

Alleluia: Second Timothy 1: 10

R. Alleluia, alleluia.

10 Our Savior Jesus Christ has destroyed death and brought life to light through the Gospel.

R. Alleluia, alleluia.

Gospel: Mark 9: 14-29

14 And coming to his disciples, he saw a great multitude about them, and the scribes disputing with them.

15 And presently all the people seeing Jesus, were astonished and struck with fear; and running to him, they saluted him.

16 And he asked them: What do you question about among you?

17 And one of the multitude, answering, said: Master, I have brought my son to thee, having a dumb spirit.

18 Who, wheresoever he taketh him, dasheth him, and he foameth, and gnasheth with the teeth, and pineth away; and I spoke to thy disciples to cast him out, and they could not.

19 Who answering them, said: O incredulous generation, how long shall I be with you? how long shall I suffer you? bring him unto me.

20 And they brought him. And when he had seen him, immediately the spirit troubled him; and being thrown down upon the ground, he rolled about foaming.

21 And he asked his father: How long time is it since this hath happened unto him? But he said: From his infancy:

22 And oftentimes hath he cast him into the fire and into waters to destroy him. But if thou canst do any thing, help us, having compassion on us.

23 And Jesus saith to him: If thou canst believe, all things are possible to him that believeth.

24 And immediately the father of the boy crying out, with tears said: I do believe, Lord: help my unbelief.

25 And when Jesus saw the multitude running together, he threatened the unclean spirit, saying to him: Deaf and dumb spirit, I command thee, go out of him; and enter not any more into him.

26 And crying out, and greatly tearing him, he went out of him, and he became as dead, so that many said: He is dead.

27 But Jesus taking him by the hand, lifted him up; and he arose.

28 And when he was come into the house, his disciples secretly asked him: Why could not we cast him out?

29 And he said to them: This kind can go out by nothing, but by prayer and fasting.

~

TUESDAY FEBRUARY 25, 2025

First Reading: Sirach 2: 1-11

Responsorial Psalm: Psalms 37: 3-4, 18-19, 27-28, 39-40

Alleluia: Galatians 6: 14

Gospel: Mark 9: 30-37

First Reading: Sirach 2: 1-11

1 Son, when thou comest to the service of God, stand in justice and in fear, and prepare thy soul for temptation.

2 Humble thy heart, and endure: incline thy ear, and receive the words of understanding: and make not haste in the time of clouds.

3 Wait on God with patience: join thyself to God, and endure, that thy life may be increased in the latter end.

4 Take all that shall be brought upon thee: and in thy sorrow endure, and in thy humiliation keep patience.

5 For gold and silver are tried in the fire, but acceptable men in the furnace of humiliation.

6 Believe God, and he will recover thee: and direct thy way, and trust in him. Keep his fear, and grow old therein.

7 Ye that fear the Lord, wait for his mercy: and go not aside from him, lest ye fall.

8 Ye that fear the Lord, believe him: and your reward shall not be made void.

9 Ye that fear the Lord, hope in him: and mercy shall come to you for your delight.

10 Ye that fear the Lord, love him, and your hearts shall be enlightened. My children behold the generations of men: and know ye that no one hath hoped in the Lord, and hath been confounded. For who hath continued in his commandment, and hath been forsaken? or who hath called upon him, and he despised him?

11 For God is compassionate and merciful, and will forgive sins in the day of tribulation: and he is a protector to all that seek him in truth.

Responsorial Psalm: Psalms 37: 3-4, 18-19, 27-28, 39-40

R. (5) Commit your life to the Lord, and he will help you.

3 Trust in the Lord, and do good, and dwell in the land, and thou shalt be fed with its riches.

4 Delight in the Lord, and he will give thee the requests of thy heart.

R. Commit your life to the Lord, and he will help you.

18 The Lord knoweth the days of undefiled; and their inheritance shall be for ever.

19 They shall not be confounded in the evil time; and in the days of famine they shall be filled:

R. Commit your life to the Lord, and he will help you.

27 Decline from evil and do good, and dwell for ever and ever.

28 For the Lord loveth judgment, and will not forsake his saints: they shall be preserved for ever. The unjust shall be punished, and the seed of the wicked shall perish.

R. Commit your life to the Lord, and he will help you.

39 But the salvation of the just is from the Lord, and he is their protector in the time of trouble.

40 And the Lord will help them and deliver them: and he will rescue them from the wicked, and save them, because they have hoped in him.

R. Commit your life to the Lord, and he will help you.

Alleluia: Galatians 6: 14

R. Alleluia, alleluia.

14 May I never boast except in the Cross of our Lord Jesus Christ, through which the world has been crucified to me and I to the world.

R. Alleluia, alleluia.

Gospel: Mark 9: 30-37

30 And departing from thence, they passed through Galilee, and he would not that any man should know it.

31 And he taught his disciples, and said to them: The Son of man shall be betrayed into the hands of men, and they shall kill him; and after that he is killed, he shall rise again the third day.

32 But they understood not the word, and they were afraid to ask him.

33 And they came to Capharnaum. And when they were in the house, he asked them: What did you treat of in the way?

34 But they held their peace, for in the way they had disputed among themselves, which of them should be the greatest.

35 And sitting down, he called the twelve, and saith to them: If any man desire to be first, he shall be the last of all, and the minister of all.

36 And taking a child, he set him in the midst of them. Whom when he had embraced, he saith to them:

37 Whosoever shall receive one such child as this in my name, receiveth me. And whosoever shall receive me, receiveth not me, but him that sent me.

～

WEDNESDAY FEBRUARY 26, 2025

First Reading: Sirach 4: 11-19

Responsorial Psalm: Psalms 119: 165, 168, 171, 172, 174, 175

Alleluia: John 14: 6

Gospel: Mark 9: 38-40

First Reading: Sirach 4: 11-19

11 Wisdom inspireth life into her children, and protecteth them that seek after her, and will go before them in the way of justice.

12 And he that loveth her, loveth life: and they that watch for her, shall embrace her sweetness.

13 They that hold her fast, shall inherit life: and whithersoever she entereth, God will give a blessing.

14 They that serve her, shall be servants to the holy one: and God loveth them that love her.

15 He that hearkeneth to her, shall judge nations: and he that looketh upon her, shall remain secure.

16 If he trust to her, he shall inherit her, and his generation shall be in assurance.

17 For she walketh with him in temptation, and at the first she chooseth him. She will bring upon him fear and dread and trial: and she will scourge him with the affliction of her discipline, till she try him by her laws, and trust his soul. Then she will strengthen him, and make a straight way to him, and give him joy,

18 And will disclose her secrets to him, and will heap upon him treasures of knowledge and understanding of justice.

19 But if he go astray, she will forsake him, and deliver him into the hands of his enemy.

Responsorial Psalm: Psalms 119: 165, 168, 171, 172, 174, 175

R. (165a) O Lord, great peace have they who love your law.

165 Much peace have they that love thy law, and to them there is no stumbling block.

R. O Lord, great peace have they who love your law.

168 I have kept thy commandments and thy testimonies: because all my ways are in thy sight.

R. O Lord, great peace have they who love your law.

171 My lips shall utter a hymn, when thou shalt teach me thy justifications.

R. O Lord, great peace have they who love your law.

172 My tongue shall pronounce thy word: because all thy commandments are justice.

R. O Lord, great peace have they who love your law.

174 I have longed for thy salvation, O Lord; and thy law is my meditation.

R. O Lord, great peace have they who love your law.

175 My soul shall live and shall praise thee: and thy judgments shall help me.

R. O Lord, great peace have they who love your law.

Alleluia: John 14: 6

R. Alleluia, alleluia.

6 I am the way and the truth and the life, says the Lord; no one comes to the Father except through me.

R. Alleluia, alleluia.

Gospel: Mark 9: 38-40

38 John answered him, saying: Master, we saw one casting out devils in thy name, who followeth not us, and we forbade him.

39 But Jesus said: Do not forbid him. For there is no man that doth a miracle in my name, and can soon speak ill of me.

40 For he that is not against you, is for you.

~

THURSDAY FEBRUARY 27, 2025

First Reading: Sirach 5: 1-8

Responsorial Psalm: Psalms 1: 1-2, 3, 4 and 6

Alleluia: First Thessalonians 2: 13

Gospel: Mark 9: 41-50

First Reading: Sirach 5: 1-8

1 Set not thy heart upon unjust possessions, and say not: I have enough to live on: for it shall be of no service in the time of vengeance and darkness.

2 Follow not in thy strength the desires of thy heart:

3 And say not: How mighty am I? and who shall bring me under for my deeds? for God will surely take revenge.

4 Say not: I have sinned, and what harm hath befallen me? for the most High is a patient rewarder.

5 Be not without fear about sin forgiven, and add not sin upon sin:

6 And say not: The mercy of the Lord is great, he will have mercy on the multitude of my sins.

7 For mercy and wrath quickly come from him, and his wrath looketh upon sinners.

8 Delay not to be converted to the Lord, and defer it not from day to day.

Responsorial Psalm: Psalms 1: 1-2, 3, 4 and 6

R. (40:5a) Blessed are they who hope in the Lord.

1 Blessed is the man who hath not walked in the counsel of the ungodly, nor stood in the way of sinners, nor sat in the chair of pestilence.

2 But his will is in the law of the Lord, and on his law he shall meditate day and night.

R. Blessed are they who hope in the Lord.

3 And he shall be like a tree which is planted near the running waters, which shall bring forth its fruit, in due season. And his leaf shall not fall off: and all whatsoever he shall do shall prosper.

R. Blessed are they who hope in the Lord.

4 Not so the wicked, not so: but like the dust, which the wind driveth from the face of the earth.

6 For the Lord knoweth the way of the just: and the way of the wicked shall perish.

R. Blessed are they who hope in the Lord.

Alleluia: First Thessalonians 2: 13

R. Alleluia, alleluia.

13 Receive the word of God, not as the word of men, but as it truly is, the word of God.

R. Alleluia, alleluia.

Gospel: Mark 9: 41-50

41 For whosoever shall give you to drink a cup of water in my name, because you belong to Christ: amen I say to you, he shall not lose his reward.

42 And whosoever shall scandalize one of these little ones that believe in me; it were better for him that a millstone were hanged around his neck, and he were cast into the sea.

43 And if thy hand scandalize thee, cut it off: it is better for thee to enter into life, maimed, than having two hands to go into hell, into unquenchable fire:

44 Where their worm dieth not, and the fire is not extinguished.

45 And if thy foot scandalize thee, cut it off. It is better for thee to enter lame into life everlasting, than having two feet, to be cast into the hell of unquenchable fire:

46 Where their worm dieth not, and the fire is not extinguished.

47 And if thy eye scandalize thee, pluck it out. It is better for thee with one eye to enter into the kingdom of God, than having two eyes to be cast into the hell of fire:

48 Where their worm dieth not, and the fire is not extinguished.

49 For every one shall be salted with fire: and every victim shall be salted with salt.

50 Salt is good. But if the salt became unsavoury; wherewith will you season it? Have salt in you, and have peace among you.

∽

FRIDAY FEBRUARY 28, 2025

First Reading: Sirach 6: 5-17

Responsorial Psalm: Psalms 119: 12, 16, 18, 27, 34, 35

Alleluia: John 17: 17b, 17a

Gospel: Mark 10: 1-12

First Reading: Sirach 6: 5-17

5 A sweet word multiplieth friends, and appeaseth enemies, and a gracious tongue in a good man aboundeth.

6 Be in peace with many, but let one of a thousand be thy counsellor.

7 If thou wouldst get a friend, try him before thou takest him, and do not credit him easily.

8 For there is a friend for his own occasion, and he will not abide in the day of thy trouble.

9 And there is a friend that turneth to enmity; and there is a friend that will disclose hatred and strife and reproaches.

10 And there is a friend a companion at the table, and he will not abide in the day of distress.

11 A friend if he continue steadfast, shall be to thee as thyself, and shall act with confidence among them of thy household.

12 If he humble himself before thee, and hide himself from thy face, thou shalt have unanimous friendship for good.

13 Separate thyself from thy enemies, and take heed of thy friends.

14 A faithful friend is a strong defence: and he that hath found him, hath found a treasure.

15 Nothing can be compared to a faithful friend, and no weight of gold and silver is able to countervail the goodness of his fidelity.

16 A faithful friend is the medicine of life and immortality: and they that fear the Lord, shall find him.

17 He that feareth God, shall likewise have good friendship: because according to him shall his friend be.

Responsorial Psalm: Psalms 119: 12, 16, 18, 27, 34, 35

R. (35a) Guide me, Lord, in the way of your commands.

12 Blessed art thou, O Lord: teach me thy justifications.

R. Guide me, Lord, in the way of your commands.

16 I will think of thy justifications: I will not forget thy words.

R. Guide me, Lord, in the way of your commands.

18 Open thou my eyes: and I will consider the wondrous things of thy law.

R. Guide me, Lord, in the way of your commands.

27 Make me to understand the way of thy justifications: and I shall be exercised in thy wondrous works.

R. Guide me, Lord, in the way of your commands.

34 Give me understanding, and I will search thy law; and I will keep it with my whole heart.

R. Guide me, Lord, in the way of your commands.

35 Lead me into the path of thy commandments; for this same I have desired.

R. Guide me, Lord, in the way of your commands.

Alleluia: John 17: 17b, 17a

R. Alleluia, alleluia.

17b, 17a Your word, O Lord, is truth; consecrate us in the truth.

R. Alleluia, alleluia.

Gospel: Mark 10: 1-12

1 And rising up from thence, he cometh into the coasts of Judea beyond the Jordan: and the multitudes flock to him again. And as he was accustomed, he taught them again.

2 And the Pharisees coming to him asked him: Is it lawful for a man to put away his wife? tempting him.

3 But he answering, saith to them: What did Moses command you?

4 Who said: Moses permitted to write a bill of divorce, and to put her away.

5 To whom Jesus answering, said: Because of the hardness of your heart he wrote you that precept.

6 But from the beginning of the creation, God made them male and female.

7 For this cause a man shall leave his father and mother; and shall cleave to his wife.

8 And they two shall be in one flesh. Therefore now they are not two, but one flesh.

9 What therefore God hath joined together, let not man put asunder.

10 And in the house again his disciples asked him concerning the same thing.

11 And he saith to them: Whosoever shall put away his wife and marry another, committeth adultery against her.

12 And if the wife shall put away her husband, and be married to another, she committeth adultery.

REFLECTIONS

REFLECTIONS

VERSION INFORMATION

About the Douay-Rheims 1899
American Edition Bible

The **Douay-Rheims Bible** is a treasured translation of the Holy Scriptures that has long been revered within the Roman Catholic tradition. Originally translated from the Latin Vulgate, the Douay-Rheims Bible was produced by English-speaking Catholic scholars in the late 16th century. The New Testament was first published in Rheims, France, in 1582, and the Old Testament followed in Douai, France, in 1609-1610.

The **1899 American Edition** represents a significant milestone in the history of the Douay-Rheims Bible. This edition, printed in the United States, was carefully revised to enhance readability while preserving the rich, traditional language that characterizes this translation. Known for its formal and dignified prose, the Douay-Rheims Bible provides a faithful rendering of the Scriptures as they were understood within the Catholic Church for centuries.

As the most widely used English Catholic Bible prior to the 20th century, the Douay-Rheims holds a special place in the spiritual life of English-speaking Catholics. It is cherished not only for its historical significance but also for its deep connection to Catholic teachings and liturgical practices.

In this book, we present the timeless words of the Douay-Rheims Bible, allowing the sacred texts to continue to inspire and guide the faithful.

Whether you are a lifelong devotee of this venerable translation or encountering it for the first time, we hope that these readings will deepen your understanding of the divine mysteries and enrich your spiritual journey.

∽

BOOKS OF THE BIBLE

OLD TESTAMENT

Genesis
Exodus
Leviticus
Numbers
Deuteronomy
Joshua
Judges
Ruth
1 Samuel
2 Samuel
1 Kings
2 Kings
1 Chronicles
2 Chronicles
Ezra
Nehemiah
Tobias (Tobit)
Judith
Esther
Job
Psalms

Proverbs
Ecclesiastes (Qoheleth)
Song of Songs (Canticles)
Wisdom
Ecclesiasticus (Sirach)
Isaiah
Jeremiah
Lamentations
Baruch
Ezekiel
Daniel
Hosea
Joel
Amos
Obadiah
Jonah
Micah
Nahum
Habakkuk
Zephaniah
Haggai
Zechariah
Malachi

~

NEW TESTAMENT

Matthew
Mark
Luke
John
Acts of the Apostles
Romans
1 Corinthians
2 Corinthians
Galatians
Ephesians
Philippians
Colossians
1 Thessalonians
2 Thessalonians
1 Timothy
2 Timothy
Titus
Philemon
Hebrews
James
1 Peter
2 Peter
1 John
2 John
3 John
Jude
Revelation

❧

Nativity with Saint Francis & Saint Lawrence (1599)
Michelangelo Merisi da Caravaggio

CONCLUSION

This concludes Book One
Other books in the series encompassing
Liturgical Year C include:

BOOK 2:
Mar, Apr, May
BOOK 3:
Jun, Jul, Aug
BOOK 4:
Sep, Oct, Nov

Made in United States
Orlando, FL
05 December 2024

54975453R00143